DATE DUE

AP 24 '00			
MY 17 '00			
JE 1 0 '00			
AP 21 '03			

DEMCO 38-296

NEW FRONTIERS IN HISTORY

series editors

Mark Greengrass

Department of History, Sheffield University

John Stevenson

Worcester College, Oxford

This important new series reflects the substantial expansion that has occurred in the scope of history syllabuses. As new subject areas have emerged and syllabuses have come to focus more upon methods of historical enquiry and knowledge of source materials, a growing need has arisen for correspondingly broad-ranging textbooks.

New Frontiers in History provides up-to-date overviews of key topics in British, European and world history, together with accompanying source material and appendices. Authors focus upon subjects where revisionist work is being undertaken, providing a fresh viewpoint which will be welcomed by students and sixth-formers. The series also explores established topics which have attracted much conflicting analysis and require a synthesis of the state of the debate.

Published titles

C. J. Bartlett
Defence and diplomacy: Britain and the Great Powers, 1815-1914

Jeremy Black
The politics of Britain, 1688-1800

Paul Bookbinder
Weimar Germany: the Republic of the reasonable

Michael Braddick
The nerves of state: taxation and the financing of the English state, 1558-1714

David Brooks
The age of upheaval: Edwardian politics, 1899-1914

Carl Chinn
Poverty amidst prosperity: the urban poor in England,1834-1914

Conan Fischer
The rise of the Nazis

T. A. Jenkins
Parliament, party and politics in Victorian Britain

Keith Laybourn
The General Strike of 1926

Panikos Panayi
Immigrants, minorities and British society, 1815-1919

Daniel Szechi
The Jacobites: Britain and Europe, 1688-1788

John Whittam
Fascist Italy

Forthcoming titles

Joanna Bourke
Production and reproduction: working women in Britain, 1860-1960

Ciaran Brady
The Unplanned conquest: social changes and political conflict in sixteenth-century Ireland

Susan-Mary Grant
The American Civil War and Reconstruction

Evan Mawdsley
The Soviet Union 1922-1956

Alan O'Day
Irish Home Rule

David Taylor
Crime, conflict and control: the advent and impact of the New Police

Europe after Napoleon

Europe after Napoleon

Revolution, reaction and romanticism, 1814–1848

Michael Broers

Manchester University Press

Manchester and New York

Distributed exclusively in the USA and Canada by St. Martin's Press

Copyright © Michael Broers 1996

rom the British Library

Library of Congress Cataloging-in-Publication data
Broers, Michael.
    Europe after Napleon: revolution, reaction and romanticism/ by Michael
Broers.
        p. cm.
    Includes bibliographical references (p.).
    ISBN 0-7190-4722-6. — ISBN 0-7190-4723-4 (pbk.)
    1. Europe — History — 1815-1848. I. Title.
    D383.B68 1996
    940.2'82—dc20   95-47221

ISBN 0 7190 4722 6 *hardback*
ISBN 0 7190 4723 4 *paperback*

First published 1996

00 99 98 97 96   10 9 8 7 6 5 4 3 2 1

Printed in Great Britain
by Bell & Bain Ltd, Glasgow

Contents

Acknowledgements

My first debt is to the editors of the *New Frontiers* series, Dr Mark Greengrass and, in particular, Dr John Stevenson, who encouraged me to write this volume. The staff at MUP have been efficient and tolerant to an unwarranted degree, and special thanks are owed to Jane Thorniley-Walker, Vanessa Graham, Michelle O'Connell, and Carolyn Hand, who saw it all through! I take great pleasure in having the opportunity to praise the staff of the Brotherton Library of Leeds University, and to acknowledge the greatness and riches of that institution. Particular thanks are offered to my friends there, Neil Plummer and Nicola Holmes. A considerable debt is also owed to the staff of the John Rylands Library of Manchester University. Together, these two institutions and their staff enrich living and working in northern England. My deepest thanks go to my friend and former colleague, Dr Toby Abse and, above all, to my wife, Sue, who together over a curry in Bradford, convinced me to 'get on with it'. I hope they were right!

Introduction

Few periods of modern history are as baffling as the years between the fall of Napoleon in 1814 and the end of the revolutions of 1848–51. Historians are generally agreed that these decades form a distinct era in European history, but they are seldom sure as to why. Even the appropriateness of the usual tag attached to this era – the Restoration – is open to dispute. A close examination of the work of the Congress of Vienna shows that the 'restoration' was less about particulars than circumstances. Boundaries and even dynasties were less important than a more general restoration of peace and stability. Indeed, Paul Schroeder has argued convincingly that what emerged in 1814–15 was not a restoration at all, but a wholly new system of international relations and, up to a point, domestic politics.[1]

The title of the standard textbook of the period by Jacques Droz – *Europe Between Revolutions*[2] – probably conveys more than its author intended, for Droz sees these decades as completely shaped by the legacy of the French Revolution, as little more than a postscript to greater, more seminal events. To Droz, the period 1814–48 is also the antechamber to the Industrial Revolution. He argues that the combination of these new forces and the political legacy of the French Revolution produced the conflagration of 1848; it was all just a matter of time; those who lived through these years were little more than the prisoners of the past and the helpless hostages of a rapidly emerging future. No new ideas emerged in these years; politics consisted solely of attempts by reactionary governments to repress the new ideas engendered by the Revolution, in their doomed efforts to put back the clock. The system was held together by the brute force of the Holy Alliance for as long as

1

possible until, by 1848, 'the old Europe of the 1815 treaties was no longer anything but a worn out facade'.[3] This vision could not be further from that of Schroeder, who sees the essence of the 'Vienna System' as a force for stability and peace, but even more, as durable, outlasting the trauma of 1848: 'Only the Vienna settlement got things right; only it established peace.'[4]

There are also great disputes over the significance of the internal political life of the European states in this period. Where Droz sees only repression and a struggle between the old order of the eighteenth century and the more recent – but still old – order of the Revolution and Napoleon, others discern the opening of a new political, social and economic world. Paul Johnson has seen in the 1820s and 1830s 'the birth of modernity'.[5] Perhaps more soberly, the Italian historian Adolfo Omodeo – writing first under the shadow of war and fascism in 1940 and then in the shattered but hopeful Europe of 1945–47 – saw in the Restoration a period of humanity and retrenchment. He saw the period as a flowering of civilisation in its widest sense, in a political world that, whatever its faults, granted Europe the time and peace to develop the arts and sciences. In constitutional states such as France, a modern, vibrant political life was given the time denied it during the Revolution, so laying the foundations for a freer, more humane future. To Omodeo, the Restoration was something of a 'silver age', something to cherish and remember in the darkest hours, as well as to turn to for inspiration, in the post-war years.[6]

There is great truth in all of these definitions of the period. The present author sees Schroeder's assessment of the international settlement as correct; it provided a stable, far from oppressive framework within which domestic political life might evolve. The domestic histories of the period are more problematic for the historian, however. The extremes of interpretation are embodied in the attitudes of Droz and Omodeo. To reject that of Droz is to ignore the seething hatreds below the surface of public life in Europe, hatreds which dated back to the Revolution, if not beyond it. They were a fact and a dread spectre for all contemporaries. However, to embrace this view wholeheartedly, is tantamount to admitting that political life remained unchanged for a generation. Conversely, to accept the thesis of Omodeo without equal reserve, is to believe that the new age actually did dawn, that the past was laregly left behind.

The truth would seem to lie less between these two extremes, than in another direction. From the heritage of the Revolution – and from the pre-revolutionary order – the men of Restoration Europe forged their own, unique political culture, to confront the problems of their own times. In so doing, they had to refight many old battles, while at the same time bequeathing to future generations a political vocabulary whose major terms are still in use today. The Restoration must first be treated on its own merits, and through the study of its own preoccupations, before its place in modern European history can be grasped.

The author has come to see this era as both homogenous and unique. It developed a rich political culture of its own, no more or less rooted in the past than that of any other period. It survived in its true form during the few brief decades which saw its creation. It arose quickly after 1814, forged by the deliberate efforts of contemporary politicians and thinkers, determined to avoid the horrors of the recent past, and endured only as long as the material circumstances of the early nineteenth century lasted. By the 1840s, it was fading in most of western and central Europe under the broad impact of modernisation. The unity of the period is, indeed, its position between two revolutions, but what happened between them was influenced less by the past – or the future – than by the resolve of so many men, of vastly differing opinions, to make their own political world, for their own needs.

It would not be going too far to say that the political culture of the Restoration was the work of three generations of European men[7] – for behind all the talk of 'liberty', 'equality' and 'justice', it was a man's world – and the interaction between these three generations is central to the period.[8] It was also a world of prosperous, educated men, an elitist world. The history of Europe from the late 1780s until 1848 had been riven by massive changes: empires rose and fell, states and rulers were overthrown, with terrifying rapidity, and the net result was that those who came of age ten or fifteen years apart entered a very different world from their predecessors or their successors, and they knew it. This is not a fanciful theory dreamt up by bored academics, but reflects strongly felt contemporary perceptions. The men who held the reins of power in the first decade or so after 1814, had come of age in the late eighteenth century; their seminal experience of public life had been the French Revolution, regardless of whether they embraced its ideals, detested it, or sought to sift out the bad and retain the good it may have produced. Those who followed them were shaped by the trauma of the fall of the Napoleonic empire, and the immediate demands of the post-war world. Their great political struggle came roughly between 1827 and 1832, with the emergence of new regimes over much of western and southern Europe. They were succeeded by the first generation of politicians and thinkers who had no direct experience of the Revolution or Napoleon, and their crisis came in 1848.

Largely through these circumstances, 'youth' – at least within the ranks of the educated and propertied – acquired political and cultural connotations it had not carried hitherto. Each generation was deeply conscious of how and why it differed from the others, and this had a direct influence upon politics. In the broadest, most general terms, this period saw the preoccupations of the Revolutionary era give way to new ones among the rising generations, while the most senior statesmen of the period remained under the influence of its events.

This is not to equate political or ideological divisions with generational divides, however. The major political ideologies cut across youth and middle age. Rather, it is the case that each generation was marked by deep cultural differences which, in turn, marked their approach to politics. This centres on the greatest contemporary conflict of the age among the educated of Europe: the cultural, aesthetic battle between Romanticism and neo-Classicism. This struggle influences every page of this study, even though the terms are seldom used directly. Romanticism is a vast field, and cannot be done justice in these pages. However, its presence suffused the politics of the two generations who came of age between 1814 and 1848 to a remarkable degree.

The struggle became political, but not in strictly political terms. Spitzer, for example, notes the presence of romantic youths in both the liberal and ultra-royalist factions in France during the 1820s, and the same might apply to the bitterly divided politics of Spain in the same period.[9] There was no 'youth ideology' to unite one generation against another, but each generation conceived the ideological struggle in a different way. Culture and politics were things apart for the men of the 1790s, while for their successors, public life had become 'a political-aesthetic mission';[10] politics, cultural and personal feelings were one and the same. If the generation of the immediate post-war years saw itself as more serious, sober and sincere – more level-headed and honest – than that of the Revolution, the youth of the 1830s and 1840s believed themselves to be more altruistic, humane and 'in touch with their feelings' than their predecessors. When he founded 'Young Italy' in 1831 – and 'Young Europe' four years later – Mazzini insisted that membership be restricted to those under forty. In so doing, he reflected a major preoccupation of the age, and brought it into politics in the most direct manner possible. These factors are nebulous; they are hard to translate into direct political history, but generational differences form an essential part of the background to the history of political culture in the Restoration.

These differences seldom intruded upon practical politics, but they did colour the ideologies of the period, if in a subtle, indirect way, and the structure of the book reflects this influence. Its chapters do not move in a conventional, modern sweep from 'right' to 'left'. This is not because the terms 'right' and 'left' had no meaning for contemporaries, they most certainly did, but they were not the most crucial divisions to contemporaries, nor are they the key to understanding where power lay within the political culture of the Restoration. The chapters on 'Conservatism' and 'Liberalism' stand together because they were the ideologies of those in power for most of the period; conservatives tended to dominate politics before about 1830, liberals from 1830 to 1848. They are followed by 'Reaction' and 'Radicalism' which represent the contemporary forces of opposition to the ideologies of power and influence. Although reaction assailed the centre of power from the right, and radicalism, from the left, both were influenced by cultural considerations – and infused with romanticism – more than their entrenched rivals. Taken together, these four ideological camps make up the pillars of the political world of the Restoration; they are the creations of their own times and express its preoccupations. 'Socialism' and 'Nationalism', which bring up the rear, represent new forces, marginal to the period itself, and born of still newer sets of preoccupations derived from modernisation. They would dominate the future, but they can tell us very little about the political realities of the early nineteenth century.

The core of the book is introduced by a chapter on international relations, to set the period firmly in its context and as a reminder of the essential conditions necessary to the evolution of its political culture. It is closed with a chapter on the revolutions of the period, as an attempt to explore the workings of contemporary ideologies in times of crisis, when many of their essential characteristics emerge clearly. The revolutions of 1820–23, 1830–31 and 1848–52, together with the Carlist civil war in Spain in the 1830s are the 'stress fractures' of the Restoration period, and thus provide a means of assessing the strengths and weaknesses of its political rivalries. Opening and closing the book in this way expresses the author's belief that the period is, indeed, unique, bracketed in so far as any era of history can be, by other, distinct historical experiences, in this case the Revolutionary-Napoleonic wars and the rise of modernisation, the chief political consequence of which was the emergence of more powerful and often larger political units than those of 1814–48. The political world of these decades was extinguished by new forces and new circumstances. It did not fall from within.

Finally, there is a very concrete reason for approaching the period through its ideological themes. It stems from the battle cry of many tutors and teachers: 'Define your terms'. Experience as both victim and perpetrator has shown the author that this is easier said than done for the political world of the Restoration. The meanings of 'left' and 'right' can be obscure enough when employed in the course of a detailed narrative history; their finer distinctions are more treacherous, still. Indeed, these initial difficulties are made even greater, if the period is treated on its own terms and modern definitions become more of a hinderance than a help to the student.

There are three reasons for this confusion of terms. The first has already been stated: the lasting influence of Restoration political culture was the political vocabulary it gave modern Europe. However, it did not give later generations its discourse, the context in which its terms were used. Put more simply, terms such as liberalism, conservatism and socialism did not mean exactly what they do today, but they are close enough to be miconstrued, if not handled with care.

Secondly, the historiography of this period has been used and abused by politically motivated historians, often shamelessly. Later generations of nationalist historians, especially in Germany, Italy and central Europe, have made the initial mistake of placing nationalism and nationalist aspirations at the centre of political life, although the balance is now redressed.[11] This grave error, wilful or not, was compounded by the desire of nationalists to portray the regimes of the period as 'reactionary', unless they were clearly liberal in the sense of having representative institutions, and sometimes not even then.[12] Too often, careful terminology aimed at clarifying the politics of another era, has given way to partisan name-calling.

Contemporaries also often used terms now in current use indiscriminately, as well as for political purposes but they were, after all, theirs to use. To the embattled exiles and agitators of the 'Left', reactionaries and conservatives could melt into one, just as to the men in power, 'radicals', 'socialists' and even 'liberals' were words to induce paranoia, whatever the reality. This is only to be expected, and if the present author has imposed his own broad terms on them, it is only in an effort to reach a better understanding of their times, not to alter the complex, sophisticated and rich political world they created for themselves. That this era produced such a refined political culture, and that it has not survived into our own, is perhaps a tribute to their level of civilisation, rather than ours.

Notes

1   P. W. Scroeder, *The Transformation of European Politics, 1763-1848*, Oxford, 1994, p. 580.

2   J. Droz, *Europe Between Revolutions, 1815-1848*, first published Glasgow, 1967.

3   *Ibid.* p. 245.

4   Schroeder, *Transformation*, p. 577.

5   P. Johnson, *The Birth of Modern World Society, 1815-1830*, New York, 1991.

6   A. Omodeo, *Studi sull'Età della Restaurazione*, Turin, 1974 edn. First published 1940 and 1946.

7   The term is used in the sense of 'cohorts', to signify groups close together in age, born roughly within ten years of each other, rather than in the strictly demographic sense of a familial span of thirty to thirty-five years. See especially K. Mannheim, 'The problem of generations', in *Essays on the Sociology of Knowledge*, London, 1959 and A. Spitzer, 'The historical problem of generations', *American Historical Review*, 78, 1973, pp. 1353-85.

8   In a French context, A. Spitzer, *The French Generation of 1820*,

Princeton, 1987. For Germany, R. Elkar, 'Young Germans and Young Germany: some remarks on the history of German youth in the late eighteenth and in the first half of the nineteenth cnetury', in M. Roseman (ed.), *Generations in Conflict. Youth revolt and generation formation in Germany, 1770-1968,* Cambridge, 1995, pp. 69-91.

9 Spitzer, *The French Generation,* p. 29.

10 Elkar, 'Young Germans', p. 76.

11 Schroeder, *Transformation,* and R. Gildea, *Barricades and Borders. Europe, 1800-1914,* Oxford, 1987, are among the most notable books to debunk these myths, at the general level.

12 As Schroeder points out, similar views to those of the nationalist historians of the late nineteenth century have been reiterated in some recent studies, notably C. H. Church, *Europe in 1830: Revolution and Political Change,* London, 1983: Schroeder, *Transformation,* p. 576. fn. 84. Droz, *Europe,* has perpetuated these views long after their rejection by most scholars.

1

The context:
the Congress of Vienna and the
reordering of Europe

The Napoleonic legacy and the task of the Congress

The Napoleonic empire dominated almost all of continental Europe between 1804 and 1814. The creation of the Napoleonic state system meant the wholesale redrawing of the political maps of Italy, Germany and the Low Countries – the west as it is thought of today – as well as further flung areas such as Poland and modern Croatia. The organising principle of this empire was uniformity and, in this respect, it was very much a new kind of empire. Rarely did Napoleon annex a foreign territory and then leave its internal workings alone, as had usually been the case in European history before. Napoleonic rule usually entailed the introduction, in whole or in great part, of the uniform, highly centralised system of administration and justice that had evolved in France since the Revolution of 1789.[1] Napoleonic rule was oppressive, burdensome and usually deeply resented as an alien imposition by most of the peoples of Europe, even by the French.[2] Nevertheless, it was usually efficient and provided a coherent internal structure for the states under its control, as well as an international order focused clearly on France and French interests. Its very nature left little room for diversity of any kind. By and large, this was what the victorious allies found in place when they finally defeated Napoleon in 1814–15.

This made the task of the Congress of Vienna very peculiar, indeed. The Congress was not there to bring order out of chaos. Extremely good order prevailed in most of western Europe, outside Spain, and there are many instances of Napoleonic officials waiting patiently at their posts in Italy and Germany, before calmly handing over local administration to the advancing allies at a mutually agreed moment. Nor was it about imposing a uniform settlement on

9

the rulers it restored after the fall of Napoleon. Different monarchs were restored under very different terms, to the point where the usefulness of the term 'restoration' itself is often rightly brought into doubt by historians. In some areas, such as those parts of the Rhineland which passed under Prussian rule, or Lombardy which was restored to Austrian rule, the administrative structures created by Napoleon were left largely untouched, whereas in Piedmont-Savoy and the Papal State, concerted efforts were made to uproot all the changes wrought under Napoleonic rule.[3] The French Bourbons were allowed to return to the throne specifically on condition that they granted a written constitution which established an elected, representative form of government. This was enshrined in the Charter of 1814. In contrast, their Spanish and Neapolitan cousins were allowed to disregard similar advice and ruled without any formal checks on their power. Such was the variety of 'restorations' effected in 1814–15.

The reordering of Europe by the Congress of Vienna was exactly about recreating diversity by overturning an efficient, uniform political order and this makes its task intriguing to the historian. The territorial settlements made by the Congress were remarkably enduring; most of the borders agreed on in 1814–15 survived into the mid-nineteenth century almost unaltered. This was a considerable accomplishment in itself, particularly when set against the uncertainties which beset the states of Europe in the eighteenth century – whose limited, dynastic wars hinged on the redistribution of territory – and the bitter nationalistic quarrels of the twentieth century. However, the Congress established, not quite inadvertently, a still more fundamental change in the ways relations between states were conducted. Diplomatic relations were no longer governed by dynastic, almost personal concerns. Treaties now assumed a genuinely legal status and no longer depended on the dictates of individual rulers; they were made by and for states, not ruling houses. Dynastic and territorial disputes still occurred, indeed they were particularly frequent in the years immediately after 1814, but they no longer escalated into wars. As a result, these principles were tested almost as soon as they were conceived, and were found acceptable.[4] Whereas before 1814, the Great Powers used such disputes between lesser states as vehicles for their own ambitions, in the post-Vienna order of things, they worked to keep them apart. Thus, the first essential factor for an understanding of the period 1814–50, is the new international context in which its domestic history took place: international security was better guaranteed than at any time before or since in the history of modern Europe, through the legalised treaty system, backed by the active intervention of the Great Powers – Russia, Prussia, Austria and France, and Britain until 1822 – who acted with the wider consent of the lesser states.

At a different level, the Congress of Vienna ended the administrative and political uniformity that went with Napoleonic hegemony. By 1814, most of continental western Europe had behind it the shared experience of the effects of the French Revolution and Napoleonic rule. Now they were quite deliberately cut adrift from each other under profoundly different governments and their essential business settled for them by the Great Powers. Their borders and rulers thus fixed, the post-Napoleonic states of Europe were left to go their own ways.

There were limits to this freedom, of course, and they could be made brutally clear as witnessed by the revolutions and subsequent military interventions by the Great Powers. Indeed, the British government soon found these limits too narrow and left the treaty system in 1822. The four continental Great Powers now saw their role as the preservation of what they had established, by force if necessary. They were to preserve the unique integrity of each state from the reimposition of the uniform, internationalist doctrines of the French Revolution. In practice this meant that existing rulers could not be overthrown by their own subjects or an outside power, and in no circumstances could they be replaced by anything resembling the revolutionary regimes of pre-1814. An apt analogy might be the generally shared fear of any revival of fascist regimes, anywhere in Europe, after 1945. For a generation after 1814, any renewal of radical revolution on the French model was unthinkable and unacceptable to all those in power and most people outside it.

However, within these prescribed limits, the newly independent states could evolve of their own volition. The other powers did not attempt to prevent the French making modifications to the Charter of 1814, in the following decades, nor did they intervene in 1830 when Charles X was overthrown in favour of his cousin, the less traditionalist Louis-Philippe, a true test of the tolerated limits of 'the system'. Earlier in the period, although Austria was concerned when the states of southern Germany – Bavaria, Baden, Württemberg, Nassau and Hesse-Darmstadt – adopted constitutions on the French model between 1814 and 1820, no attempt was made to interfere with them.[5] Conversely, when the restored rulers of Naples, Spain and Piedmont-Savoy rejected the advice of the Great Powers to do exactly this, no attempt was made to coerce them to do so. The crux of this approach to politics was encapsulated by the policy of Metternich, the man at its centre, and especially by his approach to the role of Austria and Prussia – the two great German powers – in relation to the lesser states of the new German Confederation. The Austrian foreign minister did not see Germany as an area to be conquered, annexed or even to be coerced indirectly into imitating Austrian models of government. Instead, Metternich sought to convince them – usually in the face of unjustified suspicion by the lesser states – that the role of Austria was to conserve these states as they were or, within limits, as what they might wish to become. Moreover, this was to be achieved in partnership with Prussia, rather than in competition to her. It was a subtle approach to the ordering of states and governments, and as such can be elusive to those approaching the period with more aggressive, clear-cut models of national rivalry or mutually hostile power blocs in mind.[6] A state system predicated on accepting – and fostering – the diversity of its participants is by its very nature a delicate, intricate construct. In this case, it endured for a remarkably long time.

Cradled by an international system that provided a remarkable level of peace and security, European culture set about absorbing the lessons of the long period of war and revolution between 1789 and 1814.[7] It is no mere coincidence that the parameters and vocabulary of modern politics emerged in the years between 1814 and 1848, for in direct contrast to the fluctuations of the earlier period, the conditions of the years between the fall of Napoleon and the revolutions of 1848–49, allowed prolonged experiments in politics to take place within the states themselves. If the revolutionary era conceived the essence of modern political culture, the period 1814–50 saw it nurtured to a degree of maturity. That process began within the context of the regimes as they were established by the Congress of Vienna.

The restored regimes, 1814–23

Essentially, there were three types of regime which emerged from the Vienna settlement: those which sought to compromise with the changes wrought by the Revolution by adopting limited constitutions, the chief examples being France and the states of southern Germany; those which attempted to preserve the advances made in administration under Napoleon by retaining Napoleonic institutions while rejecting constitutional government, such as Prussia and Austria, at least in the provinces they acquired from the Napoleonic empire; finally, those states which wholly rejected the experience of the revolutionary era and sought determinedly to put back the clock – Spain and Piedmont-Savoy being chief among them.

Those states which chose the constitutional path did not deviate from it even when, as happened in Baden as early as 1819 or France in 1830, the monarchs themselves turned against the concept of parliamentary government. It may well be a vindication of the attitude of the peacemakers of 1814–15, that if reform was sanctioned initially by a ruler at the request of his subjects, it expressed a natural and legitimate recognition of the way in which that particular state should best be ruled. However, where constitutions were perceived as being forced on unwilling rulers by frustrated minorities lacking in popular support, it was time to intervene, as happened in Naples, Piedmont and Spain between 1821 and 1823. This did not necessarily indicate a categoric rejection of constitutional government by the Great Powers; France herself was just such a regime. Rather, events such as the revolutions of 1820–23 signalled to the Great Powers that government lacking a basis of consent was bound to be unstable and, therefore, a threat to the wider international order. To the power-brokers of Europe in the early nineteenth century, it mattered less how states were governed – within limits – than that they were governed in security and, preferably, efficiently.

Whereas the constitutional states remained unchanged until 1848–49, and so are easily discernable as a distinct category, many unconstitutional states swung between embracing and then rejecting a degree of reform, according to the ministers in power. Naples and the Papal State are prime examples of this vacillation. While their governments were headed by reforming ministers like Dei Medici in Naples or Consalvi in the Papal State, attempts were made to continue and preserve some of the work of the French, but their policies were then abandoned or reversed, following the revolutions of 1820–23. Above all, they sought to reintegrate the experienced civil servants who had served the Napoleonic regime, whereas more traditionalist elements in the restored governments excluded them. States of this kind were regarded, with good reason, as serious sources of instability by the Great Powers, partly because it was felt that the exclusion of able administrators led to inefficient government. Even more worrying to the Great Powers was the inherent uncertainty created in these states by such abrupt changes of policy.

Prussia and, to a lesser degree Austria, are examples of states that rejected constitutionalism – in the case of Prussia after due consideration between 1814 and 1818 – but persevered with practical reforms. Unlike Naples or the Papal State – or the constitutional monarchies – they had never been brought wholly into the Napoleonic empire and, as such, did not possess a section of their governing class tainted by collaboration with the French. This lessened the scope for political tensions considerably, but it is to the states' credit that in special cases such as the Rhineland or Lombardy – areas formerly at the centre of the Napoleonic empire – they skilfully incorporated such men into their administration.

Spain and Piedmont-Savoy represent the other end of the spectrum, for here the rejection of the Revolution and Napoleon also meant the ejection from office of all those who had served the French. In Spain, this was done with considerable violence and over 12,000 refugees fled to France in 1814, although as will be seen, many returned gradually in the course of the 1820s, first to Spain and then to office. Many among them had actually fought the French and not collaborated at all, but were harassed for their support for constitutional government. In Piedmont-Savoy the expulsion of French trained civil servants from office had serious effects, even if it was achieved without violence or enforced exile, because the kingdom had been under French rule since 1800 and a whole generation of administrators had been formed under Napoleon. Their loss created enormous problems for the administration of this important, if lesser, European state.

As is already obvious, each of these states faced a number of serious internal problems capable of undermining the established order. More than any other single factor, the problems inherited from the Revolutionary-Napoleonic period and, in some cases from the pre-revolutionary *ancien régime*, would shape the development of politics within these states. It was against this background that the restored regimes had to establish themselves.

Domestic tensions and new ideas: the background to new politics

The deepest, most intractable problem facing most governments in the early nineteenth century was the legacy of the Revolution. Its essence was the civil war created within most states between those who had supported the French and those who had remained loyal – for a host of complex reasons – to the old order. These divisions often flared into violence in the immediate aftermath of the fall of the Napoleonic empire, as has been seen in the case of Spain. France itself witnessed some of the worst excesses, during the 'White Terror' of 1815–16 which swept much of the south in the months after Waterloo, and it is equally true that large sections of the west were very tense in these months, although violence on a large scale did not erupt.[8] If these scenes were not repeated everywhere, the potential for civil war was discerned in most states. The restored regimes either had to take sides or try to steer a course between them. This was the essential stuff of political life in the first two decades at least of the period 1814–50.

On the plain of political philosophy, confrontation centred on the abstract – but basic – question of where sovereignty originated, with the people and the nation, or with the monarch and traditional institutions. In more practical, less lofty terms, this posed two important problems: how were governments to make themselves respected; that is, how could the newly restored rulers prove themselves to their subjects? How, too, in practical terms, was government to be conducted? Put another way, where did authority really lie in constitutional states like France or Baden and would retaining so many Napoleonic institutions actually compromise the claim of restored governments to legitimacy, instead of strengthening them as so many reformers claimed? The search for answers to these basic problems launched the awesome experiment in politics that characterises the early nineteenth century.

The essence of the early years of the Restoration is the search for legitimacy and stability after the traumas of the Revolutionary era. For those at the helm of state, it amounted to the search for a solid basis of consensus through which to carry on the work of recuperation, to establish at least a few unquestioned assumptions about authority. Before this could happen, the divisions of the recent past had to be overcome. In France, this was attempted by direct compromise; in Spain and Piedmont, by explicit rejection of one side of the quarrel. Almost everywhere else, rulers sought different routes at different times. All of them were haunted by the spectre of failure, for this is the most striking lesson the experience of the Revolution and Napoleon had taught contemporary monarchs. Their deepest fears were not really that the Revolution would rise again to overthrow them – an international order had been created to prevent that – and by and large it did. The Revolution had shown them that they or their predecessors had failed to manage their own affairs, that no certainties about the present could be imported safely from the world of the *ancien régime* into that of the Restoration. This set many unlikely candidates among the restored rulers along the path of reform.

Three major models for a new basis for sovereignty emerged from the conflagration of the revolutionary-Napoleonic period, all of which challenged traditional concepts of absolutism, but none of which were easily reconciled with each other.

The first new model was Napoleonic-style 'enlightened authoritarianism', a derivative of enlightened absolutism. It is mistaken to regard this form of government as unconstitutional or purely arbitrary. In contemporary terms, constitutional states were not necessarily states with representative assemblies or even written constitutions. The constitutionalism of enlightened absolutism was a matter of governing by and within a clearly defined legal framework, which bound the state and its officials as well as the subject. This concept of legalism – 'the well ordered police state'[9] as it has been aptly termed – was widely accepted by 1814, even by rulers who were deeply opposed to representative government, notably the Habsburgs. This system rested on a very powerful centralised state, staffed by a more or less meritocratic elite drawn from nobles and non-nobles alike, but not directed by them. This lack of truly representative institutions – as opposed to a consultative process – was a major reason why Napoleonic-style rule had struck no deep roots in Europe. It failed to give political power to those propertied, influential people it chose to rely on most.

The second political model was Jacobin-style popular democracy, based on the principles of the stillborn Constitution of the Year III in France, the constitution drawn up by Robespierre and his adherents that was torn up after he was overthrown. Its central tenet was universal manhood suffrage, and its prime importance for the politics of the early nineteenth century was its affirmation of the principle of popular sovereignty, without which no regime was legitimate in the eyes of those who advocated it. It found a powerful, even more popular echo in the Spanish constitution of 1812, which had also been abortive. The political system expressed by these constitutions was formally anathema to the Vienna system. They were the essence of subversive politics in the early nineteenth century and most revolutionary leaders appealed to one or other of these constitutions, at various times.

The third model might best be termed British-style parliamentarianism, and it found a powerful following among the propertied classes of continental Europe. It provided a workable framework for a representative – but still elitist – form of government which previous models, such as the French constitution of 1791, had not set out as definitively. For those frightened by the results of the French Revolution, but still anxious to retain some of its gains, this seemed the way forward. Alongside the monarchy was an elected lower house and an openly elitist upper chamber. This model could accommodate itself easily to the institutions of monarchy and aristocracy, at least in theory, for it was predicated on the existence of both, the former to act as the executive, the latter to comprise all or part of the upper house of its legislature. In a period when concepts of authority were confused and in a state of flux, this seemed to offer the hope of combining traditional sources of authority with the political aspirations of the propertied classes. These hopes underlay the Charter of 1814 in France and, up to a point, the constitutions of the southern states of Germany. An experiment along these lines had already taken place in Sicily, during the last years of the Napoleonic wars and its suppression by the Bourbons in 1815 was deeply resented by the elite of the island.[10] The drawing power of the British model attains still more influence in those cases where such comparisons were not wholly apt. The Prussian provincial estates and the supporters of the restoration of traditional noble estates of many smaller German states sought to portray these bodies as fulfilling the same role as a British-style legislature, claiming to be both representative and traditional.[11] Herein lay its greatest chance of success.

However, perhaps the most unexpected shock the restored rulers faced was that, alongside the new divisions of the Revolution, many older sources of tension re-emerged after 1814. They, too, had to be confronted and the unfinished business of the old order posed a vital threat to the restored regimes. Another powerful political tradition had emerged from the revolutionary era which rejected all these models: reaction. The Great Powers were better equipped to protect their creations from the revolutionary enemy they had fought for so long than from more traditional sources of opposition to the state. That opposition was much closer to power than the beaten, hunted revolutionaries, however, and in the immediate context of 1814, it posed the greater threat to stability. The political education of modern Europe begins here.

Notes

1   G. Ellis, *The Napoleonic Empire*, London, 1991. S.J. Woolf, *Napoleon's Integration of Europe*, London, 1990.

2   On the French state: I. Woloch, *The New Regime. Transformations of the French Civic Order, 1789-1820s*, London, 1994.

3   On the Rhineland: J. Diefendorf, *Businessmen and Politics in the Rhineland, 1789-1834*, Princeton, 1980. On Lombardy: R.J. Rath, *The Fall of the Napoleonic Kingdom of Italy, 1814*, New York, 1941.

4   Schroeder, *Transformation*, pp. 575-81.

5   R. D. Billinger, *Metternich and the German Question. States' Rights and Federal Duties, 1820-1834*, Newark, 1991, pp. 52-5.

6   *Ibid*, pp. 171-8.

7   A view shared by Omodeo, *Studi*, who speaks of Europe 'reposing in the womb-like peace of the Holy Alliance', pp. 13-14.

8   On the south: B. Fitzpatrick, *Catholic Ultraroyalism in the Department of the Gard, 1814-1852*, Cambridge, 1983. On France as a whole: R. S. Alexander, *Bonapartism and the Revolutionary Tradition in France. The Fédérés of 1815*, Cambridge, 1991.

9   See M. Raeff, *The Well Ordered Police State: Social and Institutional Change through Law in the Germanies and Russia, 1600-1800*, New Haven, 1983, best articulates the concept.

10   J. Rosselli, *Lord William Bentinck and the British Occupation of Sicily*, Cambridge, 1956.

11   R. M. Berdahl, *The Politics of the Prussian Nobility. The development of a conservative ideology, 1770-1848*, Princeton, 1988.

2

Conservatism: the ideology of power

The problems of definition

Conservatism was the political ideology of those in power in most European states early in the Restoration period. As such, it was the ideology of practical politics and diplomacy, with all the compromises and complications this entailed. It expressed itself in deeds and policies, not abstract theories. This can make conservatism fluid and hard to define, but in contemporary terms, it also makes it important to understand. The other ideologies of the period defined themselves with reference to conservatism, usually in opposition to it. Conservatism was the practice of power.

Its practical nature meant that conservatism travelled under many names, some of them quite confusing. This, itself, is almost a political issue among historians. Nationalist and leftist historians often label conservative politicians as 'reactionary', to a degree that is unhelpful for a realistic understanding of both the domestic politics and diplomacy of the period.

It is almost as misleading to portray them as 'liberals', although this is more understandable, particularly in parliamentary states. This has led to conservatives being labelled 'conservative liberals' or 'dynastic liberals', and to confusion between the terms 'Right' and the 'centre-Right'. Broadly, conservatives are synonymous with the 'Right', as distinct from the 'centre-Right' - the most moderate, cautious branch of liberalism - or the 'Ultra Right', the reactionaries. Generally, conservatives had more in common with liberals than with reactionaries, but there were crucial differences between them which are explained best by an examination of their attitudes to key, concrete issues of the day.

Conservatism continued to evolve; it could not be static, given its central place in politics, and this adds to the confusion of how best to define it. Although always at odds with true reactionaries, conservatives at the centre of power were often prepared to make concessions to them, especially when reaction centred on a powerful nobility or strong provincial interests. They were often bound together by a common fear of revolution; they were almost always on common ground in the defence of the institutions of monarchy, the established church, aristocracy, and the tangible force of dynastic loyalty, as distinct from the more abstract concept of monarchy. However, there were important exceptions even to this basic list, as revealed by the examples of the Carlist wars in Spain, and the acrimony between the Sicilian barons and the Bourbons in Naples.

In time, the experience of the French Revolution became more remote, and consequently, it became harder for conservatives to work with reactionaries as the regimes they controlled began to incorporate liberals and liberal policies, gradually at first, but often in a calculated fashion. This process can be seen at work in Spain, when in the last decade of Ferdinand VII's rule, from the end of the revolution of 1820-23 until his death in 1833, he quietly reintegrated many exiled or disgraced liberal politicians. This culminated in the amnesties of the last years of his reign and then the swift introduction of constitutional rule in 1834, after his death. The alliance between conservatives and reactionaries, forged after the scare of the revolution in 1823, dissolved in the next decade, under the pressures of practical administration.

In Italy, Consalvi and Dei Medici learnt the same lessons even sooner. The experience of Cardinal Consalvi, chief minister of the Papal States for most of the period 1814-23, is a good example of the yawning gap that could separate conservatives from reactionaries. Consalvi, with the support of Metternich, sought to preserve many of the administrative and financial reforms begun in the 1780s under the reforming Pope Pius VI, and intensified under Napoleon. Parliamentary government was anathema to Consalvi, but he feared his state would become unviable without a measure of practical reform. However, he met ferocious opposition from reactionary cardinals, the *Zelanti*, who, like the Spanish reactionaries in these years, regarded any borrowings from Napoleonic or enlightened ideas as treasonable. Indeed, they caused Consalvi far more trouble than the much feared *Carbonari*. However, after the deaths of Consalvi and Pius VII in 1823, their successors in office, even though elected as supporters of the *Zelanti*, soon learned the same hard lessons in government. They returned, piecemeal, to the path of reform, encountering much the same opposition.[1] In Naples, Dei Medici confronted similar problems. His experience of the Sicilian constitution of 1812 turned him against any form of representative government, but he was anxious to continue not only many of the reforms of the Napoleonic decade, but to include many of its prominent servants in his administration, alongside those enlightened reformers who had accompanied the court into exile in Sicily. This policy of 'amalgamation', together with his determination to centralise and strengthen the state at the hands of the great barons, earned him the enmity of the reactionary Count Canosa, who Dei Medici had banished from the kingdom at one stage, and the secret society which formed around Canosa, the *Calderari*. Like Consalvi, Dei Medici received strong support from Metternich, but ultimately, he was unable to master the tide of reaction.

Although it is inaccurate to undervalue the ideological differences between conservatives and liberals, the main source of division in the first years of the Restoration was frequently their roles in the immediate political past. Liberals had served Napoleon or been more open to the ideas of the French Revolution, and readier to subordinate them to native reforming traditions than conservatives, who usually put dynastic or national loyalties above ideological preferences. Liberals, then, were tainted with collaboration; conservatives, who had often worked closely with them before the 1790s, were not - and therefore found themselves in power in 1814. The road back for the liberals was longer and more fraught. As time healed the wounds, so the distinctions blurred. Where they failed to fade, as in France, so the divisions persisted and, indeed, intensified.

Conservatism did not so much stand between reaction and liberalism on a political kaleidoscope running neatly from right to left; rather, it defined itself from both of them in a complex series of relationships. Conservatives, as those in power, defined those relationships. It was at their behest that liberals and liberal ideas were adopted or rejected. It was they who held the reactionaries at bay or formed a common front with them, as necessary. The Prussian bureaucracy held the powerful forces of *Jünker* reaction in check, while also controlling liberal elements - even within its own ranks - without seriously alienating either, surely one of the greatest political achievements of the period. Liberals remained loyal to a state with a reforming tradition, reactionaries were blackmailed by appeals to dynastic loyalty, thus preventing the emergence of openly hostile camps at the heart of the state.

In almost every state of the period, parliamentary or absolutist, conservatism and conservatives were synonymous with the state and with political power. As such, conservatism influenced its rivals more than it was affected by them. They were the targets of revolution and counter-revolution, and the source of authority that had to be reckoned with. Until about 1830, their grip on power was indisputable; after the revolutions of that year, it is arguable that the triumphant liberals evolved in a conservative direction.

Conservative reform in practice

(i) Politics and the State: the absolutist heritage
Conservatives were the direct heirs of the reforming ministers of enlightened absolutism. Many were, in fact, servants of the pre-revolutionary order, such as Metternich and Montgelas, the chief minister of Bavaria. Both began their careers under the enlightened absolutism of Joseph II and Leopold II of Austria and they remained men of the Enlightenment, with a deep belief in rationality and order. Yet they feared the excesses of the Revolution and after 1814, they were less confident that there was a universal model for government, or that reform could be enacted without some compromise with tradition. Stability could now outweigh the benefits of reform.

Conservatives were far from uniform in their attitudes to reform, but there were common strands that were of greater importance than the details of political life. At the heart of conservatism stood the concept of what Marc Raeff has called 'the well ordered police state'.[2] This was both a governing principle and an ideal to strive after. Its roots stretched back beyond enlightened absolutism, to the Carmeralist thinkers of the early eighteenth century. It demanded first and foremost, that the internal administration of the state be run according to strict, formalised rules which governed all concerned, from the monarch to the lowest rung of the civil service. The state could make the rules - with or without a degree of public participation - but it had to be bound by them.

In practice, this meant that the pivot of government became the civil service, which was to be staffed with highly educated, highly trained bureaucrats whose first loyalty was to the public good. This common purpose was what would cement the bureaucracy to the monarch and to society as a whole, hopefully making irrelevant the awkward theoretical problems of national versus dynastic sovereignty thrown up by the French Revolution.

This view gained a powerful grip on the Prussian bureaucracy, which came to see itself almost as a caste apart, charged with the care of the state and society. When questions about the introduction of representative institutions arose in the early nineteenth century, they felt that the most important function of representation was to ensure that they, themselves, were those represented, as it was their views that would shape the fate of the state. To this end, either through elected bodies or written, carefully regulated but absolutist constitutions, they sought to set themselves - and the state - at the centre of power. The Prussian minister von Hardenberg, might support the central liberal ideal of a representative constitution, but only if it was subordinate to a powerful civil service. When his plans for a constitution of this kind were frustrated - in part by Metternich - von Hardenberg developed in its place, the *Staatsrat*, a royal council composed of senior administrators and magistrates which a contemporary described as 'an intra-administrative parliament'.[3]

A similar attitude to the nature of the state - but interpreted in a more traditional manner - dominated the thinking of Francis II of Austria. Francis was categorically opposed to representative institutions in his domains, but distinguished himself from despotic rulers in his own eyes - and in the eyes of those who served him - by strict adherence to legal formalities. Whether through constitutions or professional bureaucracies, conservatism meant the rule of law derived from rational, enlightened precepts, by a powerful, centralised state.

Most *ancien regime* states were polyglot by nature, and the task of the enlightened absolutists had been to reduce them to a degree of legal and administrative uniformity, a process Napoleonic regimes continued. Many of the states to emerge from the Vienna Settlement were even more heterogeneous in nature, as still more new territories were added to the *ancien regime* polities. In the first decades of the nineteenth century, when Prussia acquired large parts of the Rhineland, Piedmont-Savoy, the old Republic of

Genoa, or Baden, a swathe of territories from other German states, the old administrative problems of the eighteenth century were reborn in a more acute form. These problems of diversity influenced the responses of conservatives to the new sets of questions arising about representative institutions in the post-revolutionary world.

Few conservatives were hostile to the concept of a limited constitution, but in practice, this depended on how it would affect the unity and uniformity of their respective states. The integrity of the state and the monarchy was paramount to those in search of order and stability in these decades. Whereas liberals and radicals set greatest store by the existence of elected, representative institutions, conservatives looked first to the stability of states and rulers. Although stability could only be achieved through the rule of fair, enlightened laws, only authority could guarantee the rule of law, and only stable states could sustain such authority. This was the principle of Metternich's diplomacy translated into domestic politics. It was also the common ideological strand which united the varied responses of conservatives to the demand for representative institutions, and what marked them out from both liberals and reactionaries.

There were always concrete reasons, beyond the fear of revolution and quite alien from despotic power hunger, that made some regimes reluctant to grant constitutions, usually problems of the *ancien regime* that remained unsolved after the Revolutionary and Napoleonic interlude.

In Prussia, although many conservatives were sympathetic to representative institutions, most bureaucrats felt it was more important to press ahead with practical reforms, for which they needed the support of the crown against the *Jünker* interest, than to stand firm over holding Frederick-William III to his promise to grant a constitution, made in 1810. The civil service continued to wage its legal battle against the *Jünkers*, to reduce and, eventually, to destroy serfdom. Educational reforms continued apace until by mid-century over 80 per cent of the school age population was being schooled. Throughout these years, the Prussian universities were also among the best - and best funded - in Europe. Economic reforms, such as the creation of the *Zollverein*, were also the work of this unparliamentary regime.

A not dissimilar attitude prevailed in the ranks of the Tory governments of Lord Liverpool, in the very different context of the well established parliamentary regime in Britain. Here, suspicion of parliamentary reform and Catholic Emancipation were rooted partly in a Tory belief that to challenge the crown on these issues - on which George III and the Prince Regent held strong views - would diminish its place in politics, which would constitute an unwelcome change to the essence of the constitution. This attitude led many ministers otherwise favourable to such reforms to drop their requests, much as von Hardenberg did in Prussia. Backbenchers if not leading ministers, felt that Catholic Emancipation would undermine the confessional character of the British state, an important source of unity in their eyes.[4] Nevertheless, these years witnessed many important reforms in the financial and economic life of the country, under the auspices of 'ministerial technicians' like Huskisson and Robinson, in the absence of a true continental bureaucracy.

The small Italian Duchy of Parma was ruled from 1814 to 1847 by Marie-Louise, the estranged wife of Napoleon I and the daughter of Francis II of Austria. Marie-Louise proved to be as authoritarian and adverse to representative government as her father, and probably more so than her ex-husband, but she was a more determined reformer than either, particularly in the field of education. Until the student-led revolution against her, in 1831, Marie-Louise lavished funds and attention on the prestigious university of Parma, which she refounded after Napoleon had abolished it in 1805. Although she became unresponsive to new ideas after the rather petty rising of 1831, Maria-Louise turned her efforts towards primary education during the 1830s and 1840s. As a result, her policies produced levels of literacy in the region unheard of in the rest of Italy. Parma is a striking example of how conservative rule was often combined with practical reform. Marie-Louise was also a very popular ruler, outside a narrow circle of nationalist intellectuals.

Elsewhere, reasons other than the need for compromise between a reforming bureaucracy and a monarch cautious of his authority, governed the rejection or circumscription of representative institutions. As has been seen, Metternich and Francis II were often insistent that some monarchs grant constitutions on their restoration, but only in circumstances where they felt - rightly or wrongly - that their subjects had become so habituated to French-style rule, or to older, indigenous forms of representation, that it seemed a natural compromise. Hence, they imposed this condition on the restoration of Louis XVIII to the throne of France and strongly advised Ferdinand VII of Spain and most of the Italian rulers to follow his example. However, it was not something they entertained in their own domains, nor that they welcomed in the states of the German Confederation. The reasoning of Francis II was that of traditional absolutism: power belonged solely in the hands of the bureaucracy with the emperor at its head. He distrusted even his own brothers and the armed forces, seeing an absolute monarchy as the only means by which so polyglot a state as his could be held together. Metternich tended to agree with him, not from a reverence for traditional practices - for he floated projects for substantial administrative reform from time to time – but rather from more contemporary fears of the forces of revolution and incipient nationalism.[5]

Something Metternich himself failed to grasp, when he urged parliaments on the Spanish and Italian courts, was that many of Francis's own worries also affected them. The unity of states like Piedmont-Savoy or the Kingdom of the Two Sicilies, was at least as fragile as that of the Austrian Empire. Ferdinand II, in Naples, had already endured life as a parliamentary monarch while exiled in Sicily between 1811 and 1814. The experience had convinced him less that elective assemblies were the gateway to Jacobinism, than a modern, streamlined vehicle for aristocratic privilege to assert itself against the rights of the central government. The Sicilian parliament became a platform for regional separatism - and a block of Sicilian deputies in any wider assembly of the whole kingdom were unlikely to behave differently. The parliament was also a powerful lobby against the modernisation and reform of the state along centralist lines. Charles-Albert IV and Charles-Felix, in Piedmont, entertained similar fears about the separatist aspirations of the Genoese, nobility and commoners alike. To opt for a unicameral legislature was unthinkable, given its revolutionary connotations, but to adopt a more moderate constitution along British lines, with an upper house packed with nobles and - as the experience of the Sicilian elections of 1812 and 1813 showed - a lower house controlled by their clients, simply opened the door to the old demons of provincial separatism, overpowerful barons and an impotent central government. This was why even the most reform-minded ministers of these monarchs - Prospero Balbo in

Piedmont and Dei Medici in Naples - always stood by their monarchs over this issue.[6] It was also what separated them from the liberals, who shared so many of their other ideas about government. Perhaps the case that proves these rulers correct in their fears, is that of the United Kingdom of the Netherlands, where the House of Orange grudgingly granted a limited constitution in 1814, only to see the Catholic populations of Belgium use it as a platform to break away from Dutch rule by 1831.

Where powerful sectional interests were present, or a powerful nobility still unshorn of its privileges, representative institutions were seen as a danger to the priority of every ruler, the territorial unity of the state. To reformers bred in the school of eighteenth-century absolutism, representative assemblies often had more in common with baronial diets than revolutionary mob rule. They were perceived as placing a crucial barrier between the state and the individual citizen, a cherished goal of absolutist reformers. As will be seen, this was an objective shared by most liberals, but at the outset of the Restoration period its achievement was interpreted in very different ways.

Where liberals and conservatives would find common ground in the years ahead, was the belief in a highly centralised state, run by a powerful, professional bureaucracy, through a standard system of justice, finance and administration. This embraced equality of justice and taxation, with no exemption on grounds of local, noble or corporate privilege; a common language for public affairs; and freedom of trade and profession. For conservatives, even in parliamentary states, these goals remained the priority, and elective institutions were seen as a means to this greater end.

(ii) Conservatism in a Liberal System: the constitutional states
The only constitutions conservatives regarded as valid, were those granted by sovereign rulers. No other road to elective government was permissible in their eyes. Implicit in this, was a deeper belief that the legislature was always, ultimately, subordinate to the ruler. It could prove a crucial difference with the liberals, in a crisis.

The rulers of the south German states adopted constitutions for exactly the same reasons as Dei Medici and Frederick-William III rejected them. The rulers of Württemberg, Bavaria, Nassau, and Baden, were faced with newly acquired territories, full of ex-Imperial Knights, nobles who had been petty but sovereign princes in their own right, and numerous towns with special privileges. In these cases, where there was little fear of popular revolution and where the educated classes were little influenced by the French Revolution, elective institutions were used in an effort to undercut the forces of reaction. They tightened the unity of the state, bringing all sources of authority together at the centre, which suited the monarchs, and - because civil servants were permitted to serve as deputies - it also further empowered the liberal bureaucracy. In Baden, civil servants imbued with liberal ideas seized the opportunity to forge an alliance with the crown by which they won a remarkably liberal constitution, in return for helping the Grand Duke to curb the forces of reaction, intent on reclaiming their privileges. Here, the many contradictions inherent in constitutional monarchy were never severely tested, at least from inside the system.[7]

The role of conservatives in the French constitutional monarchy is more complex. Conservatives might best be designated as those who were hostile to the Revolution because they felt it had failed to bring political stability to the country, rather than for many of its reforms. They had no problem adapting to the centralised, professional administrative system created by Napoleon, nor were many of them unhappy about the re-establishment of parliamentary government.

However, one of the central problems of the constitutional monarchy was the relative importance of the crown and the elected chambers. Conservatives were much less inclined to want to test it than either the liberals or the reactionaries. They were inclined to support the reactionaries - the Ultras - over particular issues which affected religion or the financial position of the nobility, while refusing to follow them in attempts to resurrect the privileges of the *ancien regime*. Ultimately, it proved an impossible balance to strike, but only when the monarch himself, Charles X, seemed to reject the concept of constitutional monarchy. Although they agreed with his interpretation of the Charter - that the king was sovereign, not the chambers - they did not feel that his position was threatened by the electoral defeats they suffered between 1827 and 1830.

Whereas in the states of southern Germany - as in Britain since 1688 - the question of where ultimate authority lay in the state remained dormant, in France, the fears and suspicions stemming from the Revolution eventually narrowed the issue to its essentials. When many conservatives left politics altogether after 1830, it was not through a sentimental loyalty to the Bourbons, but from a deeper conviction that only the legitimate dynasty could provide the authority to make a constitutional regime work. Villèle was converted to parliamentarianism, while for many liberal aristocrats disillusioned by the Revolution, such as the Duc de Richelieu, the Charter symbolised a dream recovered. They sought to bring liberals, reactionaries and conservatives together in support of the Charter. Their specific cause was a failure, but they helped to entrench the great certainty of French liberalism, that a powerful, centralised state could cohabit with a vibrant parliamentary system.

Conservative governments and liberal political economy

In the storm of ideological differences and revolutions of the Restoration period, there was one broad area of consensus. Politicians and statesmen, from Charles X to the neo-Jacobins, from Metternich to Mazzini, accepted the essence, if not always the details, of the doctrines of the liberal economics developed by Adam Smith in the late eighteenth century and refined for the post-revolutionary generation by Say, in France, and List, in Germany. Only reactionaries and the nascent socialists stood opposed to these basic economic doctrines, which centred on free trade at home - if almost never abroad - freedom of profession and commerce and a commitment to modernise, invest and expand all branches of economic life. In practice, this meant an assault on the exclusionist privileges held by the nobility, the guilds, certain towns and provinces, an end to internal customs' barriers,and to the price fixing of essential commodities. All this was to be replaced by a free market, the world of *laissez-faire*.

This study cannot enter into a discussion of the economic life of Europe in the early nineteenth century, but even in the context of politics, it is important to remember that the European economy was still predominantly rural, even in its most industrialised, economically advanced areas, Britain and the Low Countries. Industry was advancing to a degree where it was attracting the attention of governments and investors, but most of the reforms undertaken and discussed in these decades centred on agriculture and the commerce and industries it spawned.

Although liberal economic theory looked forward to an economy free of state intervention and left to self regulation, in practice, liberals soon learned that the obstacles left behind by the old regime could not be swept away without the active intervention of a powerful state. Even when this was achieved, it became equally obvious that a general lack of capital for investment in modern technology - not primarily in manufacturing equipment, but in infrastructure, especially railways and canals - could only be realised with the help of the state. This paradox was resolved for liberals because most conservative governments embraced the central tenets of liberal economics, but injected into them the absolutist traditions of state supervision which even the most doctrinaire liberal economists saw as necessary, at least in the early stages of modernisation. In political terms, this put conservative regimes at the helm of liberal economic agendas.

Conservatives and liberals agreed over three basic concepts that linked economics to politics: the sanctity of individual property and its importance in defining the individual's place in society; the need for a free internal market; and the need for that market to operate in uniform, efficient monetary and financial conditions.

The concept of private property became central to both the liberal and conservative views of politics. For conservatives, it defined the individual as a citizen, without corporate or personal privileges; it was an essential condition for the establishment of a unified, centralised state. For liberals, and for conservatives who accepted representative institutions, property was the defining quality for participation in public life. This doctrine reached its apogee in the Spanish constitution of 1845, the work of the Moderate Party. At its formal installation, one deputy proclaimed to cheers, that 'poverty was a sign of stupidity'.[8] With marginally more tact, Guizot told Frenchmen of the 1840s that the way to expand the electorate was to *enrichez-vous*. To both conservatives and liberals, the sanctity of private property was synonymous with the rule of law, the essential human right they were both pledged to guarantee.

The concept of the internal free market was the economic equivalent of the unified, centralised state. To conservatives, it was yet another way to bind the state together and to replace local autonomy with central control. To many liberals, this was a small price to pay for free trade. The rulers of the *Mittelstaaten* of southern Germany found this aspect of liberal economics particularly useful in their concerted efforts to unify their states. Conservative governments, in partnership with liberal parliaments, took this a step further, by providing state support for building railways when it proved beyond private enterprise. In Baden, in 1838, the government undertook to build a very difficult railway from Mannheim to the Swiss border. As the chief minister told the diet, 'The government is convinced that this road is much, much too important to turn over to free management without considering the interests of the totality and preserving it with the greatest of care,'[9] a good summary of the relationship of conservatism to liberal economics.

The goal of stable, national currencies and good financial management was pursued by many conservative regimes, with liberal support and it underlined the importance of efficient government to a wide spectrum of those in political life. This was particularly urgent in the first years of the Restoration, when many countries were still suffering the effects of the Napoleonic wars. Financial policy was a central issue that turned Spanish conservatives against reactionaries in the decade after 1823, and led them to help many liberals back into politics.

In France, the sound financial policies of Villèle were an important source of unity between centre-right and centre-left. Indeed, although Charles X finally deviated from almost every principle of liberalism by the time of his fall in 1830, his image as a reactionary should not disguise his strict adherence to *laissez-faire* economics. Although he tried to revive the practice of 'touching for the king's evil', his romantic medievalism did not extend to the revival of fixing the price of grain in times of dearth. His refusal to break with liberal orthodoxy on economic matters alienated popular support for him in 1830, while to the liberal and conservative deputies in the chambers, it was simply taken as a fact of political life. Reactionaries, on the other hand, expected rulers to be 'the protector of the weak, the king of beggars, the saviour and patron of the popular masses,' in the words of the Prussian commentator Wagener.[10] When confronted by the economic demands of many reactionaries, even Charles X emerges as an orthodox liberal, as did most conservatives.

Prussia became an internal free trade zone in 1818, while Württemberg and Bavaria formed a free trade agreement in 1828.

The Prussian free trade area extended steadily during the 1820s and merged with the southern states in 1834, to become the *Zollverein*, the largest free trade area in Europe. Ironically, this most liberal of measures was greeted with considerable reservations in the diets of the south German states, because liberals there feared domination by an authoritarian Prussia. In Baden, it was the conservative government that pushed the motion for membership through the diet, by forty votes to twenty-two, in 1834.[11] Conservative zeal for liberal economics was not tempered by political considerations in most of Germany, however. Although later nationalist historians saw the beginnings of German unification in the *Zollverein*, its original purpose was to strengthen the individual German states, and that is why conservatives supported it.[12]

The fundamental importance of liberal economics to almost the whole political world becomes apparent when conservative regimes failed to embrace economic liberalism, either through a lack of resources to intervene in the economy effectively, or through political atrophy. The Spanish governments of the 1830s and 1840s made concerted efforts to foster economic growth in a liberal framework, but could not match the resources of Prussia, for example, and railways made much slower progress in Spain than elsewhere. Circumstances were different in the Italian states, however. Here, conservative rulers were reluctant to create an Italian version of the *Zollverein*, despite widespread support for the ideas of the liberal professor of political economy at Milan, Carlo Cattaneo who proposed a free trade area - devoid of political connotations - in northern and central Italy. The refusal of the Austrian government to allow a railway to be built between Venice and Milan was the catalyst for a hardening of opposition to the regime in the 1830s and 1840s.[13] Even within its heartland, the Austrian state did little to promote economic modernisation, thus slowly turning many disparate liberal interests against it.[14] Liberals soon became aware of the importance of conservative support for their economic goals, when it was absent.

In 1827, the government of Villèle attempted to restore an element of primogenitor into the French laws of inheritance laid down by the Revolution and unaltered in 1814. The government coupled this with what many - wrongly - interpreted as an attempt to confiscate *biens nationaux* and restore them to their original owners. In this attempt, Villèle stumbled upon the fork in the road that could divide conservatives from liberals. In his desire to create a more stable ruling elite through the restoration of primogenitor, Villèle provoked a clash between stability and uniformity - legal equality - and in his seeming desire to reverse the land settlement of the Revolution, he touched the untouchable, the sanctity of private property.

At this point, the natural instincts of conservatives were to turn towards stability and make exceptions to the rule, in the search for legitimate authority. They saw in such policies a deeper, more lasting guarantee of a society based on property, and the logical culmination of this as the creation of a special status for the most propertied. Liberals adhered to the concept of uniformity, and balked at the notion of any special privileges. In the terms of hard, political realities, Villèle was on his way to political oblivion. Nevertheless, the concept of property as the defining element in politics was common to all concerned. Villèle based his new elite on those families who paid the most taxes, not on the antiquity of their titles. Conservatism shaded into liberalism; increasingly, however, it was sharply defined from reaction, the defence of the old order.

Notes

1   A. J. Reinerman, *Austria and the Papacy in the Age of Metternich*, 2 vols., Washington, 1979 and 1989. S. C. Hughes, *Crime, Disorder and the Risorgimento: The politics of policing in Bologna*, Cambridge, 1994.

2   M. Raeff, *The Well Ordered Police State: Social and Institutional Change in the Germanies and Russia, 1600-1800*, New Haven 1983.

3   R. M. Berdahl, *The Politics of the Prussian Nobility. The development of a conservative ideology, 1770-1848*, Princeton, 1988, pp. 189-90.

4   J. C. D. C. Clarke, *English Society, 1688-1832*, Cambridge, 1985.

5   E. Radvany, *Metternich's Projects for Reform in Austria*, The Hague, 1971.

6   G.-P. Romangnani, *Prospero Balbo, intellettuale e uomo di stato, (1762-1837)*, 2 vols., ii, Turin, 1990, on Piedmont. R. Romeo, *Il Risorgimento in Sicilia*, Bari, 1950 on Naples.

7   L. E. Lee, *The Politics of Harmony. Civil Service, Liberalism and Social Reform in Baden, 1800-1850*, Newark, 1980.

8   Cited in R. Carr, *Spain, 1808-1939*, Oxford, 1966, p. 238.

9   Cited in Lee, *The Politics of Harmony*, p. 167.

10   Cited in H. Beck, 'Conservatives and the Social Question in Nine-

teenth Century Prussia', in *Between Reform, Reaction and Resistance: Studies in the History of German Conservatism from 1789 to 1945*, L. E. Jones, J. N. Retallack, eds, Providence and Oxford, 1993, pp. 61-94, 91.

11 Lee, *Politics of Harmony*, pp. 167-8.

12 Sheehan, *German History*, p. 434.

13 P. Ginsborg, *Daniel Manin and the Venetian Revolution of 1848-49*, Cambridge, 1979.

14 P. Judson, *German Liberalism and Nineteenth-Century Austria: Clubs, Parties and the Rise of Bourgeois Politics*, Columbia University PhD. dissertation, 1987.

3

Liberalism:
the ideology of property

Few political terms have been so used and abused as liberalism, but the early nineteenth century saw its first, clear definition as a political term, but it had a meaning specific to its own time.

Contemporaries and historians used alternatives for 'liberal' or applied it loosely with 'radical' or 'conservative', according to the specific context under discussion. Liberals and radicals might be lumped together as 'progressives' – usually against reaction – while liberals and conservatives are sometimes described as 'moderates' when in conflict with radicals or socialists. Indeed, two of the greatest political organisations of the nineteenth century were the Moderate Party and the Progressive Party, in Spain. They worked together in a political system very close to the liberal ideal. Thus, they shared its core of beliefs, but shaded off at their extremes, the Moderates towards conservatism, and the Progressives into radicalism. In Britain, a similar trajectory places the liberalism of Russell between the reforming conservatism of Grey and the Whigs – moderates – and the radicalism of Brougham's faction – progressives.

Historians of Restoration France often refer to the liberals of the Bourbon monarchy, before 1830, as the centre-Left, placing them between the conservatives of the centre-Right – most notably Richelieu, the first chief minister under the Charter, and Martingac, the last such – and the radicals, outside parliamentary politics.[1] After 1830, during their period of power under Louis Philippe, the most influential group of liberals were known as the *doctrinaires*, because of their belief in strict adherence to the constitutional norms established by the revolutions of 1830.[2]

Thus, liberalism was pivotal in politics, and often over used as a term, especially after the revolutions of 1830 brought many liberal regimes to power.[3] The period roughly between 1830 and 1848 was a golden age of liberlism, but liberalism of a very specific kind.

The emergence of liberalism

Nuances in political terminology are very useful in understanding the complexities of politics of this period, but they must not obscure the existence of a well-defined liberal ideology.

The first consistent recorded usage of the term liberal was in the Cortez of Cadiz, in Spain in 1811, when it was applied to all those deputies and journals in favour of reform.[4] At the time, this embraced many who would later be more easily recognised as radicals, not only by historians but in their own eyes. However, the political programme which emerged from the Cortez was the core of coherent ideas which crystallised under the term liberalism during the Restoration. They centred first and foremost on a commitment to rule through a written constitution that guaranteed government through elected, representative institutions, a wide degree of freedom of expression – especially as regraded freedom of the press – the sanctity of private property, religious toleration and a regulated, open system of justice. Most of this had its origins in the early phase of the French Revolution, but it re-emerged in Spain, untainted by the later excesses of the Jacobin Terror or Napoleonic authoritarianism.

These demands also formed the core of the radical programme in the early nineteenth century, and the Cortez provides an important, early example of liberals and radicals drawing together, in the face not only of counter-revolution, but when set the daunting task of reforming a backward society. Liberals soon rejected much of the Constitution of 1812, but they were clear in their belief that a flawed system of representation was preferable to none at all, in direct contrast to conservative reformers.

The reform projects of the Cortez reached far beyond purely political matters, to embrace administrative reform and the whole concept of what made a nation. In the years immediately before the Restoration Settlement of 1814–15, the liberal deputies of the Cortez laid a blueprint for a centralised state in which traditional regions played no part: no allowance was to be made for regional variations in law, administration, education or linguistic differences. There were to be no barriers between the central government and the individual citizen. The Cortez also sought to carry these concepts of individualism and uniformity into economic life, by insisting on complete freedom of trade within Spain, and on freedom of labour and profession.

The liberalism of the Cortez was far from original. However, in the aftermath of the Revolutionary-Napoleonic wars, its counted for more than earlier attempts at reform. The Spanish liberals sought to reform their country spontaneously from within and with direct reference to their indigenous intellectual and political culture, in defiance of Napoleon and the French Revolution. Their assertion of originality – however tenuous in reality – and their loyalty to Spanish tradition, made their version of reform part of the political world created at Vienna. The early years of the Restoration were a dynamic period for the development of political ideas, and much was added to the work of the Cortez of Cadiz, to give liberalism definitive shape.

Liberals were deeply conscious of the need to accommodate reform with the particular circumstances of their societies, and fearful that any resurgence of revolutionary extremism would undo all their plans, however practical or limited. Most liberals adapted reform to the existence of both monarchy and aristocracy equally, whilst also creating institutional barriers against radicalism. In practical terms, liberals turned away from the political terms of the Spanish Constitution of 1812: universal manhood suffrage – even when buffered by a system of tiered voting to filter out the direct influence of the lower classes as agreed by the Cortez – and the rejection of a unicameral assembly in favour of an upper and a lower house. This drove a wedge between liberals and radicals for half a century. Liberalism was redefined in more precise and more conservative terms than the French Constitution of 1791, whose creators had opted for a unicameral legislature because of their pronounced hostility to the aristocracy. The final refinement of liberal constitutionalism was embodied by the French Charter of 1814, which created an upper chamber – the House of Peers – that included both noble and untitled members, together with very high property qualifications for the electorate and still higher levels for deputies. Behind this, lay the older example of Britain, itself a fundamental influence on the French Charter. By 1814, the key elements of liberal ideology were in place.

Between 1814 and 1849, liberalism acquired a clarity of purpose and a more precise identity than the use of the term by subsequent generations might indicate.

The roots of liberalism: against both Right and Left

As has been seen, liberalism could have much in common with either radicalism or reforming conservatism. With the radicals, it shared an insistence on the establishment of basic civil liberties and representative government; with reforming conservatives, a belief in the need for practical administrative reforms and regulated government. At their height, and at their best, liberal regimes were capable of incorporating radicals and conservatives into their political system, if not always into their own ranks. The British system was so admired by continental liberals for this reason. However, this very success can blur the distinct character liberalism possessed before 1848. It was an identity often gained in struggle.

The last years of Napoleonic rule saw large sectors of the propertied classes reconverted to a belief in parliamentary government. Their alliance with Napoleon had come about for two reasons. The Napoleonic state exemplified the kind of 'well ordered police state' long advocated by most eighteenth-century reformers. They were also afraid of representative government after the horrors of the Terror, whether experienced, as in France, or observed from close at hand, in the rest of western Europe. By about 1812, they had repented of this; the propertied classes of the empire now wanted an end to the war, but were unable to influence Napoleon. There was a growing realisation that reforming conservatism was not just authoritarian, but that it could not be controlled even by those whose interests it was meant to serve. The emergence of constitutionalism in Spain, at this very moment, did much to concentrate their thoughts on how to remedy this in future.

Often, these hopes were frustrated, as only a handful of states instituted constitutions after 1814, but the aspirations were by now clear. Liberalism was defining itself specifically around the demand for the granting of constitutions based on national representative institutions chosen by a small electorate, based on high property qualifications for voting and still higher levels for office. Liberals and radicals had parted company after the Terror; their breach had opened the way for Napoleon. The line between liberals and reforming conservatives, blurred under Napoleon, was now being drawn with precision. There was now a perceived need for constitutional, representative forms of government either because their absence made efficient governments too powerful – like Napoleon's or, potentially, the Prussian government, at least to its new subjects in the Rhineland[5] – or because such an absence of control allowed weak regimes to remain inefficient and unreformed, however good their intentions – as was the case in the Austrian Empire or the Papal State under Consalvi.

Above all, unrepresentative constitutions left regimes of all kinds too much scope for arbitrary, unaccountable behaviour: the lesson of recent history, for liberals, was that the 'well ordered police state' could not exist without parliamentary safeguards. Closed government, however tightly regulated, might offer sufficient safeguards to personal security and property, although the violent repressions of Ferdinand VII in Spain after 1814 were a warning against even this. However, it could never ensure that governments were responsive to the practical needs of the propertied classes. In the years immediately before and after 1814, liberals learned to fear not only reaction and radicalism, but the limitations of conservative reform.

The definition of liberalism in its early stages is well illustrated by the ideas of two men at the opposite ends of the continent, operating in very different political circumstances -the French politician and journalist Benjamin Constant, and Michael Speransky, sometime Chief Minister to Tsar Alexander I. Constant had opposed Napoleon almost from the start, as the spokesman for a minority of the French politicians who were not content to run away from parliamentary politics because of the Terror and suffered years of exile as a result. In 1814, he was rediscovered as the conscience of liberalism. He used the new, freer press laws of the Charter to great effect through his influential journals – *Le Mercure, La Minerve and La Renommée* – and a host of pamphlets, to defend the Charter, and to act as a general 'watch dog' for the civil liberties it guaranteed. The parliamentary system allowed him to pursue this role in the Chamber of Deputies in the 1820s. Constant was a figure around whom a 'loyal opposition' could and did form during the ministries of Richelieu and Villèle. He was prepared to abandon his original republicanism – not only in 1814, but again in 1830 – as well as to accept a House of Peers which sanctioned hereditary nobility, better to consolidate parliamentary government.[6]

The political *milieu* of Michael Speransky was very different. Outwardly, he was the model conservative reformer. In the early years of Alexander's reign, 1803–09, Speransky masterminded a host of administrative, judicial and financial reforms, all aimed at strengthening the Tsarist state. When Speransky spoke of change, it was in terms of a stronger, better regulated role for the ministers, a hallmark of conservative reform. However, in 1809, Speransky made public a plan for a written constitution which provided for an elected national assembly, the *Duma*, and more recently discovered private papers reveal Speransky to have held far more liberal ideas about government than expressed in his plan well before 1809. These included opposition to serfdom as an impediment to the creation of a property owning society, on which he felt a liberal regime had to stand. He fell from power in 1812 and, when he eventually returned to office in 1819, Speransky – in stark contrast to Constant – confined himself to technical, administrative reforms. Speransky was keenly aware of what separated a liberal from a conservative reformer.[7]

As time progressed, liberals identified themselves specifically as the centre of politics. Louis-Philippe, whose triumph in the July Revolution of 1830 might well be seen as the zenith of liberalism, put it into plain words in January, 1831: 'We shall seek to hold to a middle way, equally distant from the abuses of royal power and the excesses of popular power.' Under constitutional regimes, the centre proved hard to hold; in the unconstitutional states, it was often impossible to reach.

Political liberalism: the struggle for the centre

Liberals found themselves in a singular position. The importance of property to liberalism is clear. At times, the need to protect it drove them to demand major reforms, often by force of arms. Liberals were often revolutionaries with something to lose and, therefore, to defend; an awkward set of circumstances. This was the dilemma of the politics of the centre, but in many cases, although it alienated liberals from other revolutionaries, it did not inhibit them from adopting tactics more readily associated with Jacobinism.

(i) Liberals in opposition: elitism and action

As the break with conservative reform became more emphatic, especially before 1830, liberals felt themselves in opposition not only when they were under threat from repression by reactionary governments, but simply when they were without representative institutions. In unrepresentative regimes, it was no longer enough to be consulted, whereas within parliamentary systems, as in France or Britain in the 1820s, loyal opposition seemed possible, although vigilance was always needed.

In the early years of the Restoration, liberals in the truly reactionary states of Spain and the Italian peninsula thought nothing of creating secret societies, imitating the tactics of radicals like Buonarotti. The most famous secret society of all, the *Carbonari*, was full of men whose concept of representative government more closely resembled those of the French Charter of 1814 than the Jacobin democracy advocated by other, more radical secret societies such as the *adelfia*.[8] In Spain, the divisions were more marked, with radicals opting for societies like the *Comuneros* and the liberals for freemasonry. With the highly developed political life of the Cortez recently behind them, radicals and liberals knew how to avoid each other and also how to use the same methods of agitation and survival.[9] The Russian Decembrist movement, which broke out on the death of Alexander I in 1825, was also a liberal conspiracy. Its members were drawn from the same social groups as many *carbonari* – army officers, bureaucrats and young nobles – and they wanted a limited constitution.[10]

Conspiracy was not alien by nature to liberal constitutionalists, at least in states with traditions of political repression. Conspiracies are, of necessity, selective and no where is the innate elitism of liberalism better seen than in this phase of its history. This was the work of the propertied and the educated, as well as the brave. The bastions of the 'sects' were the army and the civil service, whose members had often already acquired a taste for secrecy, as well as learning, in masonic lodges. The Italian radical and nationalist, Giuseppe Mazzini saw the link between conspiracy and elitism clearly . He broke with the *carbonari* by 1831, not just because most of them did not share his prime interest, Italian unification, but out of a growing detestation of their elitism and belief in constitutions based on a restricted suffrage. Mazzini's own ideas will be discussed later, but his break with the *carbonari* says much about the general character of liberalism in this period, whether in the context of marginalised conspiracy or of ministerial office.

In 'a climate which had enough restrictions to be frustrating but not enough to cut off political life entirely',[11] liberal opposition moved away from conspiracy or never engaged in it at all. This refers to the states of the German Confederation and might also apply to some of the Italian states when under the rule of conservative reformers. In Bologna in the Papal State, during the 1840s, liberals – mainly large landowners – regrouped around the local Agricultural Society and its journal, *Il Felsineo*, both of which became substitutes for political forums. Their discussions contained a hidden political agenda around which the 'Moderate Party' developed, seeking gradual political and economic reform. In those parts of the Rhineland which passed under Prussian rule in 1814, liberalism took similar forms and centred on the defence of the civil and economic reforms achieved under Napoleon. These objectives proved possible to achieve, but the lack of representative institutions in the Prussian state made Rhenish liberals apprehensive about protecting these conditions.[12]

Observing liberalism in opposition illuminates its nature considerably. Liberalism was less the doctrine of the bourgeoisie, in a Marxist sense, than of a self defined educated elite that embraced many elements of the bourgeoisie, but hardly its entirety. The core of liberalism were provincial landowners, the civil service, the army, and intellectuals with their roots in the rationalism of the Enlightenment – noble and bourgeois alike – all of whom had come to believe that only representative institutions could rescue them from arbitrary rule and also from potential obscurity.

Liberals had an unswerving belief that they – and propertied, educated people like them – needed to be rescued from that obscurity to guide the governments of their respective states. Most of their political activities in opposition in absolutist states were confined to the local or provincial level, and many of their concerns originated in local issues. Everywhere, however, their shared goal was to break out of these restrictions through the creation of representative institutions on a national level. The backgrounds of Decazes and Villèle, the leading politicians of Restoration France, bear this out. Villèle was a petty noble from Toulouse; Decazes was the son of a provincial lawyer. Both owed their rise to the parliamentary system, for only elective politics gave them access to the centre of power.

The predilection of liberals for conspiracy when face to face with the forces of triumphant reaction or for more indirect forms of political activity in times of frustration, should not obscure the central fact that parliamentary politics was the only form of political life they regarded as legitimate. Where parliamentary politics existed, they stood at its heart, even when out of office, as the example of Benjamin Constant in France reveals. Earl Grey, leader of the Whigs, was out of office for almost the whole of his political life, from 1806 until the crisis of the First Reform Act brought him to power in 1832. When the British example was cited by liberals in other European states, this loyal patience with the processes of elective government was often what caught the eye of contemporaries. In a very real sense, the acceptance of alternating majorities, of the comings and goings of ministries, made liberals of all those involved. When the liberal ministry of Decazes lost office in 1820, it was assumed his liberal colleagues would continue to support the system created by the Charter, and they did. Perhaps more surprising was when the leader of the centre-Right, Villèle, accepted his own loss of a working majoity in the lower chamber in 1827, went to the polls, duly accepted his defeat and resigned despite retaining the confidence of Charles X. In this crucial sense, the centre-Right proved itself to be liberal, whatever its differences over particular policies with the centre-Left, whose deputies had engineered the fall of Villèle. In the constitutional states, to accept the concepts of alternation, electoral defeat and loyal opposition was the true test of liberalism. In France, between 1827 and 1830, it was what separated the centre-Right and the Right, from the Ultras. Even within the restrictive constitutional systems of the *Mittelstaaten* and Prussia, where everything possible was done by the government to restrict discussion and control the passage of legislation, liberals accepted the essence of the system.

Daniel O'Connell, the leading figure of the politics of Catholic Ireland in the early nineteenth century, offers an intriguing example of liberals in opposition. His contribution to nationalism will be examined later, but many aspects of his career shed great light on the meaning of liberalism in this period. O'Connell achieved the granting of Catholic Emancipation in 1829 through electoral pressure, but backed by the thinly veiled threat of popular insurrection in Ireland, should emancipation fail to pass. His methods in the build up to the passing of the Act are a sign that liberals were capable of exploiting popular grievances to achieve their ends with as much ruthlessness as any radical or reactionary, and O'Connell's tactics have often led to the questioning of his liberal credentials, especially by his contemporaries in the British Parliament. However, O'Connell was working for distinctly liberal ends: 'emancipation' did not involve the Catholic masses, many of whom already had the vote and thus provided O'Connell with a constituency of a kind denied to most other politicians of the time. Emancipation would give propertied Catholics the right to stand for Parliament. It was a classic liberal measure. Once installed in Westminister, O'Connell was unmoved when the terms of the First Reform Act disenfranchised large sections of the Catholic, peasant electorate. His devotion to liberal parliamentarianism has often been cited as among the reasons for the decline of his influence in Ireland by the mid 1840s.[13] Almost any means could justify the establishment of representative government.

(ii) Liberalism in power: a political world defined

When in power, most liberal regimes showed clear affinities with conservatives in their approach to practical reform. This is to be expected, given their common intellectual roots in the Enlightenment and, often, in service to Napoleon. Just as a successful liberal regime might hope to win a degree of radical support through tolerant censorship, a fair judicial system and the guarantee of what would now be termed human and civil rights, so it might hope to bring conservative reformers into parliamentary politics by a commitment to the reform of the structure of the state. When liberals failed to achieve either, they were on the narrow ground on which every elitist regime risks being stranded.

The practical reforms of most liberal regimes need not be outlined in detail, so close were they to those of the conservatives. Almost always, the political triumph of a liberal regime was followed by a renewal of administrative centralisation, the realisation of free trade – at least at home – and the pursuit of cultural standardisation through a national system of education based on a uniform language and curriculum. However, where liberal regimes might differ from those conservative reformers, and from some radical governments, was in the ruthlessness with which they pursued these goals.

Conservatives were often held in check by the need to placate reactionaries, who were sensitive about local autonomy. A good example of this was in April, 1829 in France. Martignac, the Prime Minister who replaced Villèle, presented a bill to allow a degree of decentralisation of local government by allowing the members of local councils to be elected – on a very narrow franchise – instead of appointed by the central government in Paris. It was crushed by the liberal opposition. This incident offers several wider insights into the nature of liberal regimes and the political nuances within them. It shows how the centre-Right can be distinguished from the centre-Left of liberalism, in that Martignac was prepared to concede a mild degree of decentralisation within the framework of the liberal constitution, something the centre-Left would never tolerate. The difference might seem minor, but it reveals how important the concept of a centralised state was to liberals.

In some cases, this rigid concept of centralisation could also divide them from the radicals, who often 'discovered' the popularity of localism when in opposition. This will be explored further in the next chapter, but it is worth noting in the context of better defining the nature of liberal regimes. The Spanish Constitution of 1834 was the work of the future Moderate faction, many of whom were the same men who had been moderate liberals in the Cortez of 1810–13 or who had served in the Napoleonic regime. Predictably, they made no provision for locally elected institutions. However, in 1837 the Progressives were able to force a partial revision of the constitution which, although it conceded nothing to traditional regionalism, did sanction the election of municipal councils and gave them control of the National Militia. It was a necessary concession by the Moderates and, if it was not intolerable to them, decentralisation of this kind was not part of their own programme.

Liberal regimes were often marked by their suspicion of the Church, at least in Catholic countries, even if it did not always spill over into the overt anti-clericalism of many radicals. The Belgian regime created by the revolution of 1831 is an important exception to this generalisation, as it owed its initial existence to the support of Belgian Catholics, who opposed Dutch, Protestant rule. However, the norm was a climate of distrust between liberal governments and the Catholic Church. The Vatican condemned liberalism several times. Centre-Right governments, especially those in France during the 1820s, proved more willing to bridge the gap with the Church than those of the centre-Left, but even they were careful to send avowed reactionaries like Chateaubriand as their ambassadors to Rome.

When the break came between the centre-Right of liberalism and the reactionaries, the gloves often came off: Martignac expelled the Jesuits from teaching posts in secondary education. This was not enough to save his ministry, but the centre-Left did vote with him and the bills became law. This illustrates the indifference of the centre-Right to the position of the Church in society, as well as the latent hostility borne it by the centre-Left. To the former, the Church remained a corporate body to which no privileges could safely be conceded – it was an affront to centralisation. To the latter, it was an old enemy – 'reaction at prayer' – and never to be trusted. This particular problem seldom arose in Protestant countries, at least not in such a virulent form, as the established churches were firmly under state control. In most German states, confessional divisions tended to determine political loyalties, rather than direct Church-state confrontation.[14]

After 1830, confrontation between Church and state often became more direct and less easily avoidable as the liberal regimes in France, Spain and Portugal came into their own. Even in Britain, a growing number of liberals came to favour the disestablishment of the Church of England in the wake of their success in gaining Catholic Emancipation.[15] Louis-Philippe was quite pious personally, but all those who supported the July Monarchy suspected the Church of being the strongest surviving source of support for legitimism. Even as the government encouraged the participation of the Church in works of charity and education, confessionals teemed with police spies and the notion of 'the Jesuit plot' was alive and well in the corridors of power.[16] In 1845, when a proposal by the opposition to expel the order attained a massive majority in the legislature, the government acted on it by going straight to the Vatican. Although unable to destroy the Jesuits completely, they were driven underground. It was lost on no one, of whatever opinion, that a Protestant, Guizot, eventually emerged as the pillar of the regime. Neither is it a coincidence that the intellectual champion of popular Catholicism, Lammenais, passed directly from reaction to neo-socialism, without stopping off 'in the middle', as it were.

It would be wrong to speak of a deliberate, vicious policy of persecution of the Church under either the July Monarchy in France or the liberal governments in Spain, but by the 1830s, the concept of an alliance between 'Throne and Altar' was well and truly dead in western Europe. The Moderates and Progressives in Spain renewed the assault on the regular orders, the former largely for the financial gains derived from the confiscation of their properties, the latter for more subjective reasons. In France, the July Monarchy put an end to any possibility of a restoration of such lands to the Church.

Anti-clericalism proved a convenient rallying cry within the narrow world of parliamentary politics, for it was almost guaranteed to unite liberals and radicals – however briefly – as Louis-Philippe and a succession of liberal governments in Spain were quick to learn. In a wider perspective, however, it served to cut liberal regimes off from the unrepresented rural masses.

The core of every liberal regime was parliamentary elections. Among the most important aspects of the Restoration period was that for the first time in history, the constitutional states of continental Europe settled into prolonged periods of parliamentary government, where a succession of elections could be held. Constitutions let liberalism exist in safety, even when government itself was in the hands of conservatives, as in France for most of the 1820s, and in the south German states throughout the period.

As with so much else in the political discourse of the early nineteenth century, the term *elections* can confuse more than illuminate the modern observer, if it is not understood within the context of its own times. It was not only the nature and composition of the electorate that differed from later political systems, but the conduct and significance of elections themselves.

The model for elections was provided by Britain, for the upheavals of the French Revolution had not allowed regular elections to take place under any of its various constitutions before 1795, and those which were held under the Directory, between 1795 and 1799, were notable for being annulled by those who had called them. There are two central points to make about elections in this period, and they derive directly from British norms of the eighteenth century. Voting was public, not by secret ballot, and

47

governments did not lose elections. This did not diminish their importance for contemporaries, nor did it mean that they were a hypocritical sham deployed by cynical dictatorships.

A crucial difference with Britain was that, invariably in liberal regimes, local officials were appointed by the central government. Prior to the actual elections, they used government money and resources to help candidates who were either running openly as official candidates, or designated as those whose views were closest to those of the regime. However, these victories had to be worked for, as the new parliamentary regimes could not count on the 'rotten boroughs' or even extensive 'placemen' which bolstered so many British ministries, although long serving ministers such as Villèle and Guizot, in France, or Narváez in Spain, worked hard to create patronage networks.

Liberal regimes measured success by their ability to create consensus through compromise with the local notables. The goal was not only a stable power base for the regime without recourse to coercion, but also as a means of ascertaining the opinion of the wealthiest and most influential men in the provinces in the process. This became the whole *raison d'être* of the Moderate Party in Spain, to the point that by the 1840s, some historians claim it represented nothing at all beyond local interests. Success could bring its own problems, however: in 1846, Guizot's methods of 'brokerage' produced the only clear majority Louis-Philippe ever commanded; two years later, the regime was swept from power in revolution. Elitist politics always carried the risk of a wider isolation.

In some areas, even the government knew better than to challenge vested local interests that were too strong for it. Benjamin Constant was elected for Alsace several times, without official endorsement but also, at times, without official opposition. This was also true in the case of many Ultra deputies in western France, a reactionary stronghold. More common was a nominal promise by independent candidates to support the general policies of the ministry in place, promises which could and often were broken in the course of parliamentary life. There was always an opposition, but it was usually a fluctuating one and, most of the time, the narrowness of the electorate ensured that it was of a restrained, acceptable nature.

Elections themselves were meant to be public affirmations of the consensus reached during the campaign, almost a celebration of agreement, not an expression of open hostility. Most liberal states were also monarchies, and it was still unclear to what extent open defiance of an official candidate constituted something close to treason. One mark of a liberal regime was probably that it sought not to test the issue, if defeat looked likely.

There were crushing electoral defeats, nevertheless. As has been seen, the election of 1815 in France produced a reactionary lower chamber which Louis XVIII and Richelieu thought nothing of dissolving. Nor did they shrink from amending the electoral rules to manufacture a liberal chamber in 1817. Richelieu did the same thing in 1820, to create a chamber of the centre-Right. The defeat of 1827 was a turning point, however.[17] Charles X tested the principle of the rightful expectation of governments to win elections and lost, less on the principle, but on his policies.

When liberalism had to defend itself, everything short of dictatorship was justified, but that qualification was crucial. However compromised liberal regimes became in their quest to hold the centre and to reconcile elitism, monarchy and parliamentary government, they had the lesson of Napoleon behind them, and it made them determined never to surrender the power and influence of their elective assemblies. Even the Spanish Moderates, who included many generals in their ranks, and who were made dependent on the army from the outset by the threat of Carlism, affirmed the central place of the legislature in politics.

The liberalism of the Restoration was a fragile construct, so fragile that, in a French context, it has recently been branded an impossible system, doomed to failure. The inability of French liberals to accommodate monarchy within parliamentary life has been seen as evident in the confusion of terms they used to try to describe the regime.[18] This was also the verdict of Alexis de Tocqueville, one of the greatest political thinkers produced by the July Monarchy. By the end of the revolution of 1848 and the seizure of power by Napoleon III, Tocqueville accepted the failure of the liberal experiment as the central historical theme of his times in his *L'ancien régime et la Révolution*, written in bitter disappointment and self-imposed exile, as an epitaph for a doomed political world.

This fragility was born of more than the theoretical dilemmas over the nature of sovereign authority, however. To liberals, elitism seemed the way to gathering those who mattered in the provinces together at the centre, as the surest way of ensuring 'the joining of all reasonable and intelligent opinion ... the effective, intelligent majority', as one minister of the July Monarchy put it. In practice, it often produced a self-absorbed political world which could be absurdly narrow, as in Nassau, where property requirements were so high that at one time only seventy men in the whole state were eligible to stand for election.[19] This is an extreme case, but it shows how small the political world of the liberals was, and was meant to be, whether in conspiratorial sects or at the helm of state. A recent study of the Spanish province of Soria reveals how strictly and consistently the small electorate interpreted the exclusive nature of a franchise that refused to admit not only those of insufficient wealth, but also 'any man with a lucrative profession but who, through lack of ability, cannot distinguish himself in it'.[20]

Many circumstances, often self-imposed, stifled liberalism. Chateaubriand called the Orleanists of the July Monarchy 'political eunuchs'. Elitism united conservatism and liberalism. As a result, the rest of the political world stood against them.

Notes

1   G. Berthier de Sauvigny, *The Restoration*, Philadelphia, 1966.

2   P. Rosanvallon, 'Les Doctrinaires et la question du gouvernement représentatif', in F. Furet and M. Ozouf, eds., *The French Revolution and the Creation of Modern Political Culture*, vol. III, *The Transformation of Political Culture, 1789-1848*, Oxford, 1989, pp. 411-32.

3   C. H. Church, *Europe in 1830, Revolution and Political Change*, London, 1983.

4   V. Lloréns, 'Sobre la aparición de "liberal"' *Literatura, Historia, Politica (Ensayos)*, Madrid, 1967, pp. 45-56.

5   Droz, *Liberlisme*; J. Diefendorf, *Businessmen and Politics in the Rhineland*.

6   Rosnavallon, *Monarchie Impossible*.

7   See M. Raeff, *Michael Speransky, Statesman of Imperial Russia, 1772-1839*, The Hague, 1957, for Speransky as a conservative; see J. Gooding, 'The liberalism of Michael Speransky', *Slavonic and East European Review*, 64, 1986, pp. 401-24, for the new evidence.

8   R .J. Rath, 'The Carbonary: their origins, initiation rites and aims', *American Historical Review*, 69, 1964.

9   J.-L. Comellas Garcia-llera, *El Trieno Constitucional*, Madrid, 1963.

10   W. B. Lincoln, 'A re-xamination of some historical stereotypes: an

analysis of the career patterns and backgrounds of the Decembrists', *Jahrbücher für Geschichte Osteuropas*, 24, 1976, pp. 357-68.

11 J. J. Sheehan, *German Liberalism in the Nineteenth Century*, Chicago, 1982 edn., p. 10.

12 J. Droz, *Le liberlisme rheneanne*, Paris, 1940.

13 O. Macdonagh, *O'Connell*, London, 1991.

14 J. Sperber, *Popular Catholicism in Nineteenth-Century Germany*, Princeton, 1984.

15 J. C. D. C. Clark, *English Society, 1688-1832*, Cambridge, 1985.

16 G. Cubitt, *The Jesuit Myth. Conspiracy theory and politics in nine-teenth-century France*, Oxford, 1993, which notes how it faded in the 1830s, only to resurface later.

17 S. Kent, *The Election of 1827 in France*, Princeton, 1972.

18 P. Rosanvallon, *La Monarchie Impossible, les Chartes de 1814 et de 1830*, Paris, 1994.

19 Sheehan, *German Liberalism*, p. 11.

20 Cited in M. Caballero, *El Sufragio Censitario. Elecciones Generales en Soria durante el reinado de Isabel II*, Madrid and Léon, 1994, p. 16.

4

Reaction:
the ideology of defiance

Of all the political creeds which flourished during the Restoration, reaction is the most remote from the modern mind. Reaction defined itself as backward looking, yet, arguably, it was more a product of its times than either conservatism or liberalism.

Reaction had a longer pedigree than is often assumed, and longer than many reactionaries preferred to admit. Too readily, it is assumed that reaction was born in defiance of the French Revolution; that it arose as a new ideology to challenge another new ideology. This is not so. Reaction shadowed enlightened reform before 1789, just as it continued to stalk the twin siblings of enlightened absolutism, conservatism and liberalism, after 1814. Initially, reaction sought to achieve the partnership of 'Throne and Altar'. It was always a false hope, as is revealed by its pre-revolutionary past.

The roots of reaction: anti-absolutism and counter-revolution

The perceptible beginnings of what became reaction after 1814, were in the late eighteenth century, when the aggressive centralising policies of enlightened absolutists attacked traditional rights and institutions with such verve that opposition sometimes spilled over into violence. Even where opposition remained peaceful, these reforms created bitterness among those affected by them. To reactionaries, the triumph of enlightened absolutism spelled the end of exemptions from many taxes – a privilege held not just by nobles, but by whole cities and provinces. It also saw the erosion of vibrant aspects of popular religion, with the abolition of many saints' days and their festivals, as well as the closure of many convents and monasteries, which were branded 'idle institutions' by the reformers. The end of provincial privileges could bring the threat of military conscription into these communities for the first time; often, it also led to linguistic standardisation, as central bureaucracies imposed standard French, German or Spanish on areas with their own dialects or even, as in parts of the Habsburg lands, the imposition of German on populations to whom the language was totally alien. Above all, centralisation meant the loss of the provincial diets or estates and the customary legal traditions these representative bodies sustained. These assemblies cannot really be equated with the more modern parliamentary bodies created during the French Revolution or in the Restoration period, but to contemporaries, they appeared infinitely more representative than rule by civil servants appointed by – and accountable to – only the central government.

The key elements of reaction are prefigured in the opposition to enlightened absolutism. It consisted of far more than the handful of selfish nobles, fanatical clerics and ignorant, superstitious peasants that its opponents claimed it to be. There was a strong element of truth in the caricature, but reaction would never have become so great a threat, or so popular a cause, if this had been all there was to it. These resentments embraced whole cities, with their wealthy, educated burghers and guild masters, as in the German Home Towns or the great urban centres of the Austrian Netherlands, including Brussels, Antwerp and Ghent; they took in whole provinces – Sicily, the Tyrol, Valencia – or in the case of Hungary, a whole country. Reaction became a force to be reckoned with. The warning signs for the rulers restored in 1814 were already long in place.

When the French Revolutionaries, and then Napoleon and his allies, the princes of the German *Mittelstaaten*, made many of these policies their own, they acquired these sources of opposition. They had to face it without the help of claims to loyalty based in dynastic legitimacy, an incalculable but fundamental means of keeping reactionary opposition in check. They faced this problem everywhere and all the time. In these cases, there was considerable continuity between the reaction of the *ancien regime* and that of the post-1814 period.

However, the three greatest counter-revolutions of the Revolutionary-Napoleonic period occurred in very different circumstances. The revolt of 1809 in the Tyrol, the Vendean rising of 1793–1802 in the west of France and the Spanish War of Independence, 1808–14, took place in the name of absent rulers. More importantly, they took place in the circumstances created by their absence. The rebels found it easy to rally to the cause of their legitimate rulers – the Habsburgs, Francis II in the Tyrol; the young, imprisoned Louis XVII in the Vendée; the exiled Ferdinand VII in Spain – exactly because they were absent, and because these monarchs had not yet had a chance to rule them.

Divorced from the reality of the *ancien regime*, the rebels projected their own ideal of monarchy on to these 'lost leaders'. This image is very revealing of the aspirations of reactionaries. It did not remember the monarch as a 'first servant of the state', the head of a centralised bureaucracy governing a 'well ordered police state', but as the protector and guarantor of their traditional privileges or, as they were called more often, 'liberties'. His restoration meant their restoration. It was a medieval, rather than an absolutist, concept of kingship and it was quickly deflated after 1814.

The ideology of reaction in the restoration

(i) The limits of loyalty: the throne

Louis XVIII – uncle of the young Louis XVII who died in gaol in 1797 – and Ferdinand VII differed from each other in their attitudes to the political reforms of the French Revolution. They welcomed the administrative centralisation they inherited from the Napoleonic regimes. They were more absolute – in administrative terms – than any of their predecessors, and they kept it this way. Neither restored the privileges of the Church or the nobility. Neither reinstated the provincial estates or granted any degree of autonomy to the traditional regions of the realm. Louis XVIII embraced the prefectorial system left him by Napoleon, even though he purged many of the prefects themselves, after the Hundred Days in 1815. When the elections of 1815 in France produced a sweeping victory for the reactionaries – the 'Ultras' – Louis annulled the election results and dissolved the lower chamber. In Spain, Ferdinand discarded not only the radical Constitution of 1812, but also his promise, given before he was exiled in 1808, to summon a traditional Cortez based on the old provinces and estates. Francis II, meanwhile, hardened into a 'textbook' absolutist. These monarchs had their own political tradition of absolutism and it did not correspond with the ideology of reaction.

To reactionaries, absolutism made the monarch too powerful in real terms, but the impersonality of 'the rule of law' also robbed him of his moral authority. It was moral authority that mattered to reactionaries, for practical authority ought not to rest with the state. The Swiss reactionary and philosopher, Carl Ludwig von Haller – who exercised a powerful influence over Prussian reactionaries – wrote in 1816;

> Instead of the old and hearty, paternal or lordly language, which was animated with a feeling of his own and others' rights, during the last three decades of the eighteenth century, one hears, in princely laws and publications, increasingly of civil unions, of delegated power of the people, of legal and executive authority, of state servants or public servants, of state finances and so on.

His disciple, the Prussian nobleman Ludwig von Gerlach was more direct.

> There is no more vexatious enemy of legitimate rulers... no more able ally of revolution than absolutism ... Absolutism robs the king of the brilliance of his majesty, for it strips his office of that which exalts it: that he is the servant and swordbearer of Almighty God ...[1]

Thus, the erosion of the reactionary concept of kingship had begun well before the Revolution.

The old quarrels resumed, alongside the traditional restraints of respect for legitimacy, but with the new found fear of revolution to bolster them. Perhaps the only firm bond between reactionaries and the other elements of Restoration political culture was the hope for stability they, too, invested in the return of legitimate dynasties.

In France, the Revolution of 1830 proved the greatest test of all for the dynastic loyalty of reactionaries: for several years before the fall of Charles X in 1830, the Ultra deputies in the lower, elective chamber had voted against the government on many critical occasions. Indeed, their behaviour did much to bring it down. However, when Charles was deposed in favour of the Orleans branch of the dynasty, these deputies abandoned public life almost to a man. The principle – as opposed to the day-to-day practice – of loyalty to the legitimate ruler led to the mass suicide of one of the most powerful, cohesive forces in French political life.

The power of legitimacy is illustrated, above all, by the First Carlist War in Spain, where reaction vented its spleen on both traditional absolutism and the new political world of the Royal Statute. As has been seen, Ferdinand VII made progressive concessions to liberalism in the course of the 1820s, thereby compounding the initial disappointment of reactionaries in 1814. At his death, a dispute over the succession arose between his widow, Maria-Christina – acting as regent for her young daughter, Isabel II – and Ferdinand's brother, Don Carlos. The forces of reaction rallied to Don Carlos. Whereas in France, loyalty to Louis XVIII compelled the Ultras to work through the Charter, in Spain, their equivalents – the *serviles* – did not feel obliged to accept the Royal Statute of 1834 as it was the work of a usurper. They turned to war.

(ii) Beyond loyalty: the altar.
Religion – not just the traditional rights of the Church – was central to reaction. This had not always been the case before the French Revolution, which had shaken so many certainties by its assaults on religion. Reactionaries were profoundly changed by it, not in their goals and ideals, but in their perception of where the threat to them originated. They literally repented of their complacence about the certainties of life, in the face of the power of the Revolution. The continuity of religious life could no longer be taken for granted; it had to be defended not just from the 'trimming' of enlightened absolutism, but from the destructive intentions of revolutionaries.

In common with socialists, nationalists and many radicals, but in contrast to most liberals and conservatives with their stress on the rights of the individual and the impersonal state, reactionaries saw the most frightening legacy of the Revolution as the disintegration of community, of the bonds between people. Yet, whereas these other ideologies looked to new ideas to rekindle notions of reciprocal duty and responsibility, reactionaries looked back, but they did so with new eyes.

Reactionaries almost all demanded the dismemberment of the centralised state and its replacement by the old provinces, estates and corporations. This was meant to restore the 'normal' structures of life, but reactionaries were acutely aware that a return to this system – or lack of it – could lead to the rebirth of the factional, inter-communal and caste rivalries which had characterised the public life of the eighteenth century. Reactionaries knew that these tensions would be worsened by the bitter political vendettas engendered by the Revolution and the rise of new class conflicts, brought about by industrialisation. Indeed, they were probably more attuned to some of the newer sources of social discord than many conservatives or liberals in power. This is evident in the importance of 'the social question', and in particular in the need to respond to the spread of urban poverty among the Prussian reactionaries of the *Wochenblatt* group in the 1830s and 1840s.[2]

Their ultimate solution to these dilemmas was the binding force of religion. This was as true in Protestant states like Prussia or Britain, as in Roman Catholic societies. The importance of religion for reactionaries stretched far beyond the defence of the established Church – although it always included this – to the belief that religion was the only 'social cement' capable of holding together their decentralised vision of society. The lesson they had learned from recent history was that a lasting state was a theocracy. God was more than the ultimate source of authority, He was its surest guarantor. This was the common cause which identified reactionary thinkers and set them apart from conservatives.

The battle against enlightened absolutism gave reaction its rank-and-file; that against the French Revolution provided some of its most profound thinkers: the Anglo-Irish politician, Edmund Burke; the Piedmontese diplomat, Joseph de Maistre and the French nobleman, Louis Bonald. Burke died in 1797, but Maistre and Bonald lived on into the Restoration period and they became the first major exponents of 'Throne and Altar'. Maistre and Bonald explicitly subordinated 'throne' to 'altar': God was the inspiration of valid political systems, and whereas conservatives believed that tradition proved the worth of the institutions of monarchy and aristocracy because they had stood the test of time, reactionary theorists asserted that institutions only survived long enough to become traditional because they were divinely ordained. Maistre, in particular, went further, arguing that it was impossible for men to write a constitution for themselves; it had to derive from God, over time. Similarly, these thinkers saw the law as nothing more than an unfortunate necessity, due to human sinfulness. This was a striking difference from most conservative theorists – or even Burke – who saw the law as the clearest expression of the character and political needs of a society. In sum, to the philosophers of reaction, the 'throne' was not only subordinate to the 'altar', it was viewed as purely a means to the end of a divinely ordained society. As a French historian of the subject has remarked recently, it is not only because God is dead, in terms of contemporary political systems, that makes reaction so alien to the modern mind, it is because it has no real theory of the state.[3] It did not need one.

This theory was meant to combat liberal individualism and to replace the concept of self-interest with a web of reciprocal responsibilities, based on Christian ideals. However, in the context of Restoration politics, it became a threat to the revival of the absolutist state when a new generation of politicians emerged after 1814, who translated these theories into political arguments, if seldom into practice. Reaction soon returned to its original role, of challenging the impersonal, centralised state, as well as the heritage of the French Revolution. Within states, this hinged on the battle to restore lost privileges or at least to curb reform.

Bonald, Maistre and later the Swiss philosopher, von Haller, envisaged a political order based on local communities, presided over by the 'natural' elite of an aristocracy of birth, not an elite measured by material wealth. This struck deep cords with the nobility of provincial France and Spain, who had fought against the encroachments of absolutism before the French Revolution, and now saw it revived in even stronger form, as well as among Prussian *jünkers*, stricken by economic recession and struggling to prevent the sale of their estates to rich commoners. Their emphasis on localism appealed to many communities, cities and provinces which were also threatened by the growing alliance of liberalism and conservatism, in the quest for centralisation. To all such groups, an ideology that offered freedom based on the rights of the group, rather than those of the individual, had an instant appeal.

The core of their vision of political society was the family, the fundamental social unit of a Christian society, and widely accepted as divinely ordained. It was the particular genius of Bonald to conceive of property in terms of the family – and by extension, the social group – rather than in terms of the individual. This insight gave reactionaries a traditionalist response to liberal arguments on a vital issue. Property and social stability could, they argued, be reconciled, if seen in this way. This influenced Villèle's failed attempt in

1827, to reintroduce an element of primogenitor into French law, but it was tempered by his unreactionary insistence on money as the criterion. Nevertheless, the identification of family with property entered the mainstream of conservative thought.[4]

The importance of religion to reaction revived the doctrine of Ultramontanism, which held that all Catholics owed their first allegiance to the Papacy in all things. To the followers of Bonald and Maistre, this doctrine reached far beyond the right of the Pope to administer the Church in any particular country without reference to the government – although this too remained an issue. Instead it centred on the right of the Church to dictate policy, if it so chose. As a result, reaction alienated itself from those in power who could not tolerate such constraints.

The religious element in reactionary ideology makes much of it sound alien, and often absurd, to the modern mind, but religion remained the strongest card reaction held, in terms of popular appeal. To threaten the Church was to dismantle what little public charity existed in a period of bad harvests and economic recession; it was to betray the promise of stability made to the peoples of Europe in 1814. When reaction invested familiar political structures with the comforting stability of traditional religion, it reached beyond the narrow world of liberalism and conservatism.

The reaction in action: the politics of defiance

(i) The ideology of opposition

Only in a few cases did reactionaries come close to controlling government. This is another of the many paradoxes surrounding the phenomenon of reaction, that so potent a movement achieved so little power in practice. Reactionaries were condemned, at best, to the role of loyal auxiliaries to conservative governments. It was not a position their more ambitious and able political leaders tolerated for long. As has been seen, even those most Catholic, anti-Revolutionary monarchs – Charles X of France, Ferdinand VII of Spain and Charles-Felix of Piedmont-Savoy – drew away from the true reactionaries, gravitating towards conservative and even liberal ministers. When they did so, they took many able reactionaries with them. Early in 1828, under pressure from foreign governments, Charles-Felix forced the dissolution of the *Amicizia Cattolica*, an association of reactionary, pious aristocrats. The

Amicizia counted several ministers in its ranks, but they did not stand by the leader of the association, Cesare D'Azeglio, who defiantly continued to publish its journal, *L'Amico d'Italia*. Instead, they distanced themselves from the association and kept their posts.[5]

In France, the outstanding example of this is Villèle. Villèle was a leading spokesman for Ultra views in the early restoration and a member of the ultramontane Catholic society, the *Chevaliers de la Foi*. In 1814, he wrote a pamphlet attacking the Charter and calling, instead, for decentralisation. However, as has been seen, once he became a deputy, he adapted to the parliamentary system; as chief minister from 1821 to 1827, Villèle dominated French politics. He also became alienated from the Ultras who helped bring down his ministry in 1827. In retirement, Villèle returned to reaction. He criticised Louis XVIII for giving in to the allies' demands, writing in his memoirs;

> When one reviews the series of fatal concessions ... of St. Ouen (where Louis granted the Charter in 1814), one is forced to ask how this odd contrast came about between dignity and weakness, and how the same intellect, which could predict things so correctly, could reach such a level of blindness.[6]

As has been seen in Chapter 2, dynastic loyalty was moral blackmail, used by governments to manage opposition. It took a strong character to stand against it. Men like Chateaubriand, in the parliamentary system of France, or D'Azeglio, in the absolutist state of Piedmont-Savoy, were better suited to the political wilderness than Villèle. They had the intellectual sophistication to separate day-to-day political quarrelling from fundamental issues.

There were other pressures to conform, however. Unlike radical or many liberal politicians, reactionaries could taste power if they were prepared to compromise. When reactionaries stood on their principles and chose opposition, rather than co-operation with conservative ministries, they put real careers at risk. When Chateaubriand stormed out of office in 1824, he had been the French foreign minister responsible for the successful intervention in Spain. Cesare D'Azeglio served as the Savoyard ambassador to the Papacy in 1814, on the understanding that the restored monarchy intended to be less hostile to ultramontanism than before the Revolution, but when it became clear to him that this initial goodwill was evaporating, he resigned, saying '... I would find myself in the sad state of displeasing (the King) while not remaining within the limits my conscience would prefer.'[7] It was not only philosophers who set 'altar' above 'throne', but leading politicians, as well. They were a very particular breed.

Thus, the leadership of reaction fell to men of principle, whose real gifts lay in diplomacy and in the newer arts of journalism and public debate – both Chateaubriand and D'Azeglio were impressive journalists – but not in the 'horse-trading' of government. This took its toll on the movement, but it enriched its wider influence on public life and kept reaction at the centre of politics, if not of power.

(ii) The politics of ingenuity

Reactionaries were very quick to adapt to the political world of the Restoration, even if few of them actually approved of it. They seized on the new weapons at their disposal.

The French Ultras soon learned the value of free elections and a strong legislature when they won sweeping victories in the elections of 1815, after Waterloo, only to see Louis XVIII annul them. Chateaubriand had been rather isolated in 1816, when he wrote a pamphlet praising the Charter as the best way to preserve the spirit – the honour, in his words – of the old order in a new political world. He felt that the Charter would create stable conditions in which they could be reborn after the Revolution. This was at odds with the views of those royalists who wanted the Charter abolished in 1815 and replaced by provincial assemblies.[8] However, subsequently their seventy or so deputies became the most cohesive grouping in national politics, in part thanks to the personal ties and organisational skills they had acquired through the *Chevaliers de la Foi*, to which many of them belonged. After 1824, in Chateaubriand, they also had a gifted leader who thrived in opposition. Opposition itself made them staunch defenders of freedom of the press – as long as it excluded blasphemy – and of properly contested elections.

Prussian reactionaries were also quick to see these advantages. They had always defended their provincial assemblies, believing them to be part and parcel of their traditional rights. By the 1840s, many advocated a mass electorate – voting in blocks as social groups – to produce a partnership of the monarch, the nobility and the masses to hold the state and the middle classes in check.[9] They won over the king and used the higher echelons of government, the ministries, to shape such a constitution after 1849. Dynastic loyalty was rewarded and Prussia is the closest that reactionaries and conservatives came to merging with each other, their labels almost interchangeable for historians.

Parliamentary government suited reactionaries. They could win elections and, as in 1848, the bigger the electorate, the better they fared. Parliamentarianism could stifle the liberals – they could be beaten at the polls – and curb the conservatives, by balancing the power of the executive.

However, when a threat from radical subversives was perceived, reactionaries turned the weapons of revolution on their creators, often with an ill disguised contempt for the law.

(iii) The politics of fury

The greatest political project for reactionaries, the union of 'Throne and Altar', failed and was soon seen to fail. Expelled from the corridors of power, reaction fell back on its popular roots. When it did so, the ideology of community and reciprocity became the politics of violence and intransigence.

Popular violence was a real option for reactionaries – there was a large reservoir of support for them among the lower classes in both town and country – and they resorted to it in parliamentary and absolutist states alike. It was their reply to radical plots and, where necessary, to liberal or conservative control of the official means of repression. Even in Prussia, in the wake of the attempted revolutions of 1831, the reactionary writer Radowitz proposed the use of 'hired rabble as militia against the revolution.'[10] The growing partnership between reactionaries and conservatives in Prussia made these proposals irrelevant. In 1849, the peasant conscripts of the Prussian army fulfilled this role. Elsewhere, when reactionaries felt unsure of the state, or hostile to it, they created popular militias of their own. This was the policy advocated by Canosa, first in Naples, with the *Calderari*, and then in Modena, where the Duke followed his advice.[11]

Following the liberal conspiracies of 1831 in the Papal State, Cardinal Bernetti fostered the Centurions, a semi-independent militia which may have numbered 75,000 men by 1835, in a country with less than a million inhabitants.[12] Their conduct appalled

Metternich and conservatives within the Papal regime, but the terror they inspired in liberals and radicals in the provinces convinced Bernetti and the *Zelanti* of their worth. Only when Bernetti was ousted from office, at the connivance of Metternich, did the Papal government curb the brutality of the Centurions, but it was not until the election of Pius IX as Pope in 1847 that the government dared to disband them.[13]

Royal Volunteers sprang up all over Spain during the revolution of 1820–23. Most were spontaneously reformed units from the war against Napoleon, with little organisation beyond their own areas, but bolstered by massive support within them. Although space does not allow a full examination of why reaction attracted so much popular support, in Spain in 1820–23, large sections of the peasantry were aware of ideological conflicts, if not motivated solely by ideology themselves. The peasants who fought Napoleon nine years before, welcomed the French army sent by Villèle to overthrow the rebels in Madrid. Their unity contrasted with the divisions among their leaders, the Regency of Urgel, which split into two factions that well illustrate the differences between conservatives and reactionaries. The reactionaries among the Regents supported provincial autonomy and laws – the *fueros* – while the majority were absolutists. The reactionaries won the war, the conservatives, the peace.[14]

Spain and the Papacy were weak absolutist states, who needed irregular forces to support them against even the flimsiest threat. The popular, reactionary violence in the department of the Gard, in southern France, bears a striking resemblance to Spain and the Papal State, but took place under a constitutional regime. The Gard had a large, influential Protestant community which dominated the Catholic lower classes economically and politically during the Revolution and there was a long history of vendetta between the two groups. It reappeared under the Restoration, when Catholic officials protected the popular militias, who engaged in campaigns of intimidation very like those of the Centurions.[15] In political terms, Catholics of all classes in the Gard turned to intimidation because the Protestants dominated the state administration there, showing the link between reactionary violence and exclusion from state power.

All these factors – religion, localism, dynastic loyalty, and, above all, hatred of the state born of the fear of political impotence

– drove the Carlist revolt of 1834–39 in Spain. The peasant volunteers who resisted the conscript levies of the parliamentary regime translated into bloody deeds the rage of reactionaries all over Europe at their inability to place religion at the centre of politics, to dismantle the centralised state and to preserve group privileges. Carlism had support over most of Spain, but it held out only in the Pyrenean mountains, making Don Carlos reliant on supporters of regional autonomy, despite his own absolutist views. There is a debate over the relative importance to Carlism of dynastic loyalty, regionalism and religion.[16] However, in practice, Carlism was less the epitome of pure reaction, than a blend of all its forms. Even though these disparate elements managed – barely – to co-exist, they could not deliver victory.

Popular, violent reaction remained tenacious, nonetheless. Peasant rebels and bandits helped to crush the revolution of 1848–49 in Naples and waged a guerrilla war against the liberal Italian state in the 1860s, after unification. In Spain, Carlists rose in the 1840s, and again in 1873–74; they helped Franco in the civil war of 1936–39. In France, the Gard and the Vendée elected Ultra deputies, and then neo-fascists, into the 1920s. In 1832, the Vendée rose against the July Monarchy, but the government disarmed it, easily and brutally.[17] Reaction went down fighting, and often got up again, but to no avail.

Perhaps the most paradoxical aspect of reaction to the modern observer is its cultural openness. Unlike conservatism or liberalism, reaction was imbued with Romanticism and its greatest exponents – Chateaubriand and the early Lammenais, in France; D'Azeglio in Italy; Gentz and the Schelgels in Germany – were at least as widely read as many more radical Romantics. Their style and interests were well abreast of the taste of the age and their writings did much to shape them. D'Azeglio was among the first publishers to recognise the talents of the poet and novelist, Alessandro Manzoni, destined to become the foremost novelist of early nineteenth-century Italy – and ardent nationalist, radical and opponent of Austrian rule. D'Azeglio was struck by the new, fresh quality of his verse, however, as well as by his Catholicism, and offered him space to publish in his review. When Manzoni ceased to contribute, for political reasons, it was to D'Azeglio's regret.[18] Their relationship is revealing of the cultural modernity of reaction, just as it is of the limits of a shared culture in the world of restoration politics. The isolation of reactionaries was not total. Yet, although culturally more advanced than many of their opponents, their pens were seldom mightier than the resources of modernity.

(iv) The politics of failure

Reaction is defined by its failure, but it died in many ways. In France in 1830, it committed political suicide; in Spain, by 1839, it faced military defeat, both in the name of legitimism. In Prussia, it compromised with conservatism by 1849. The peculiar government of the Papal State let the *Zelanti* cling on longer than most, yet, by 1870 the state itself was reduced to the Vatican. From behind its walls, successive popes explicitly condemned liberalism, socialism, nationalism, and *laissez-faire* economics.

The fate of the Papacy symbolises that of reaction. It demanded the rebirth of moral authority, and that was all it retained. The battle was lost for localism, privilege and the theocratic state. Henceforth, French Ultras, Italian ultramontanes and Spanish Carlists expressed their politics through Catholic piety. In defeat, its enemies feared reaction, reviving the myth of the Jesuit plot which could provoke near hysteria during the 1840s in France.[19] However, the true strength of reaction – now exhausted – was its populism. With its demise, the masses looked elsewhere to counter the elitism of conservatism and liberalism.

Notes

1 Cited in R. M. Berdahl, *The Politics of the Prussian Nobility. The development of a conservative ideology, 1770-1848*, Princeton, 1988, pp. 234-5, 255.

2 Berdahl, *Prussian Nobility*, pp. 231-63; Beck, 'Conservatives and the Social Question'.

3 G. Gengembre, *La Contre-Révolution, ou l'histoire désepérante*, Paris, 1989, p. 180.

4 Gengembre, *Contre-Révolution*, pp. 174-5.

5 C. Bona, *Le 'Amicizie': Società Segrete e Rinascita Religiosa, (1770-1830)*, Turin, 1962, pp. 449-56.

6 Villèle, J.-B., comte de, *Mémoires et Correspondance du comte de Villèle*, Paris, 1888-90, vol. I, p. 245.

7 Cited in Bona, *L'Amicizie*, p. 304, note 11.

8 B. Fitzpatrick, *Catholic Royalism in the department of the Gard, 1814-1852*, Cambridge, 1983, pp. 34-5.

9 Berdahl, *Prussian Nobility*, pp. 326-33.

10 Cited in Beck, 'Conservatives and the Social Question', p. 78.

11 W. Maturi, *Il principe di Canosa*, Florence, 1944; S. Vitale, (ed.), *Il Principe di Canosa e l'Epistola contro Pietro Colleta*, Naples, 1962.

12 A. J. Reinerman, 'The failure of popular counter-revolution in Risorgimento Italy: the case of the Centurions, 1831-1847', *Historical Journal*, 34, 1991, pp. 21-41, 27.

13 *Ibid.*

14 J.-L. Comellas Garcia-Llera, *Los realistas en el Triennio Constituciónal (1820-1823)*, Pamplona, 1958, pp. 169-75.

15 Fitzpatrick, *Catholic royalism.*

16 A. Bullón de Mendoza, *La Primera Guerra Carlista*, Madrid, 1992; see J.-C. Clemente, *Historia General del Carlismo*, Madrid, 1992, for directly contrasting views.

17 Fitzpatrick, *Catholic royalism*, pp. 183-90; P. Blois, *Les paysans de l'Ouest*, Paris, 1971; H. A. C. Collingham, *The July Monarchy: A political history of France, 1830-1848*, London, 1988, pp. 122-30.

18 Bona, *L'Amicizie*, pp. 327-41.

19 Cubitt, *Jesuit Myth.*

5

Radicalism:
the ideology of generosity

A cause of its times

Radicalism had a clear political purpose by 1814, to establish representative government based on manhood suffrage, with no property qualification for voting or holding office. To be a radical, was to believe in popular sovereignty – that authority and power derived only from the people. They saw themselves as the heirs of the French Jacobins and those deputies of the Cortez of Cadiz who supported manhood suffrage. They were the custodians of the Constitution of the Year II of the French Revolution and the Spanish Constitution of 1812, both strangled at birth. This made them inveterate opponents of reaction and conservatism.

In comparison to conservatism and liberalism, the political heritage of the radicals was clear and precise. They believed wholeheartedly in the French Revolution, but especially in the Terror; their founding text was Thomas Paine's *The Rights of Man*, written in 1789. Most were republicans, more so in France and Italy – and therefore were automatically excluded from mainstream political life – but in the German states, Britain and Spain, republicanism was not a radical priority, although few were hostile to it in theory. Radicals usually believed in centralisation and many of the other practical reforms favoured by conservative reformers and liberals, although in some cases – notably in some of the German states and Spain – they came to support elections for municipal government. Most drew the line at provincial autonomy because it threatened national unity.

The nation was the practical expression of the people, as a whole – the fusion of the state and its subjects – and the only political unit radicals regarded as legitimate. Effectively, this made all nationalists into radicals in the Restoration period but the two causes were not synonymous: radicals in Spain, Portugal, England – as opposed to Britain – and France accepted that the nation corresponded to the boundaries as they stood. Yet this is not to say that nationalism was not important to them. Radicals in these countries believed passionately in the idea of 'the nation'. Together with liberals, they valued national education, sought to foster a common language and instill the sense of a shared culture in all classes of society and in every region of the nation. The course of national unity began with the destruction of aristocratic and corporate privileges; thus, the restrictive franchise favoured by liberals was the last barrier to unity. The vote was a nationalist issue; participation in politics, an assertion of belonging.

Radicals in the Italian and German states did not always favour national unification; many saw themselves as reformers within their own, existing states – Prussia, Baden, Naples, Piedmont-Savoy – rather than nationalists as the term was coming to be understood. In these well-established states, if a radical became a nationalist, it was through personal conviction. The Venetian radicals exemplify this; when they rose against Austrian rule in 1848, most of them did so to restore the independence of the old Venetian Republic, lost in 1797, not as Italian unitarists.

However, nationalism attracted radicals in provinces and regions 'displaced' by the Congress of Vienna, or where there were long standing tensions with the central government. Thus, in those parts of the Rhineland given to Prussia in 1814 nationalism made headway among radicals as the only alternative to alien, conservative Prussian rule. There was a similar pattern in Lombardy, as Austrian rule became unpopular after 1814, and in the Legations, the province of the Papal State around the city of Bologna. Both had been part of the Napoleonic Kingdom of Italy, and so used to more autonomy than they were allowed after 1814, but neither had known real independence prior to Napoleon. In these circumstances, radicals bent on reform for local, as well as ideological reasons, were drawn to nationalism.

The relationship between radicals and socialists seemed more complex than it was. Radicals often called themselves 'socialists' – most notably the *démocrates-socialistes* in France in 1849 – but not because they agreed with socialism. Rather, it was to indicate that they cared about 'the social question', to distance themselves from the indifference of liberal regimes to social deprivation and pov-

erty. Their solution to these ills was political, however, not economic. Looking back to Jacobinism, radicals believed that manhood suffrage would ease the plight of the popular classes, not
trade unions or government intervention in the economy. They
preferred voluntary charity; those among them who were doctors
or lawyers often gave their time and skills free to those in need, or
at low cost. It was as far as most would go, however. The differences between radicals and socialists did not always seem clear
before 1848 – often they did not matter to contemporaries – but
they were real. Political radicals were economic liberals.

Radicalism belonged to an elite. It was driven by men from the
professional classes, the army, academe, and the growing ranks of
journalists. Class nuances could separate radicals from liberals,
but not class differences, and radicals knew their roots were in liberalism, if not their future. Yet in direct contrast to liberalism, it
sought to break out of that elitism. It stood out against liberalism
and socialism in its hatred of the idea of barriers between men.
This imbued radicalism with passion and a spirit contemporaries
called 'generosity'. The poet Lamartine, foreign minster of the
French Second Republic, issued a 'declaration of alliance and
friendship with all peoples.'[1] Radical spokesmen were nothing, if
not articulate. The vocation of radicalism was to transform itself
into a popular movement, but whereas reaction attracted popular
support almost naturally, radicals had to strive for it. Yet radicalism evolved into a single issue movement – the fight for the vote. It
was an issue that rose and fell between 1814 and 1848.

Radicals in power: the politics of passion

Radicals came close to power only when they seized control of the
state in a revolution, as in Spain and Naples in 1820 or when they
integrated into a secure parliamentary system, under the wing of
liberal regimes, as in Britain and Spain in the 1830s and 1840s. In
the former circumstances, their rule was brief and intense, leaving
powerful memories but few lasting achievements. In the latter,
radicals were very much the junior partners in government, exer-
cising influence, rather than real power. Even when they gained
the cherished goal of manhood suffrage, as in France in 1848–49,
radical parties did not fare as well at the polls as conservatives or
reactionaries, although they emerged as a sizeable minority in the

legislature.

Revolution or, more precisely, the *coup d'état,* suited radicals. This betrays radicalism's liberal roots: a movement bent on popular democracy was most effective when it swept opposition aside by tight knit conspiracies. The revolution of 1820 in Spain was the work of small cells of young, radical army officers in the key garrisons, organised on the same secret lines as Masonic lodges. A few months later, a similar group in Naples followed the Spanish example. Within weeks, both toppled the ramshackle royal governments. The officer corps proved, for the first of many times in modern history, that a dedicated minority could impose itself on a weak country. The Spanish and Italian rebels meant to open the way to a bright, new world. Instead, they set the pattern for thousands of future military dictatorships.

They had a clear goal, the restoration of the Constitution of 1812, but they were full of the passionate sense of a wider mission typical of radicals. Evarisro San Miguel, a rebel leader, wrote years later of 'the great movement which would so influence the destinies of Spain, began very simply. In that simplicity, was the sign of the sublime nature which marks the great deeds of great men'.[2] Their aims and hopes were simple; their methods were sly and elitist, and it was soon clear the young radicals had little popular backing outside the large cities. Once in control of the state, their lack of experience allowed more experienced liberal politicians back into power, and they soon retreated from parliamentary politics – where liberals more skilled in debate outmanoeuvred them – back to the 'para-political' world of secret societies and clubs, their true home.

The revolutions of 1820 set a major example over the tendency of liberals and radicals to co-operate in opposition, only to turn on each other in power if under pressure. The pattern was repeated in France and in the Rhineland, in 1848–49.[3] The difficulties of the liberals have been discussed; for radicals, the problem was their refusal to compromise over the democratic nature of the constitution and a commitment to intervene abroad in this cause.

In foreign policy, especially, the spirit of generosity outran realism. The ambassadors of rebel Spain agitated and encouraged Italian radicals in 1820. In Madrid, the leading radical Moreno Guerra declared that '(the revolution in) Naples is a part of us; the blood of the Neapolitans is mixed forever with that of Madrid'.[4] Noises of this kind finally provoked the great powers to crush the revolutions. French radicals took a similarly 'generous' stand in 1848, when they tried unsuccessfully to press the liberal government of the Second Republic to support the Polish revolt against Russia. Finally, as the tide of reaction rose against the liberal regimes, the radicals re-emerged to lead during the final crises, proof that their militancy was as indispensable as their politics were inept.

In power, the radicals preferred 'style' to content; their approach to victory was flamboyant. The post-coup 'street party' was their hallmark. It was a rapid switch from secrecy to transparent emotionalism, perhaps a way of compensating for their elitist methods. Public, symbolic shows of unity – of fraternity in their discourse – were deeply important to radicals when in power. They disgusted their liberal allies: in Paris in 1848, Louis Garnier-Pagès, himself a republican, said they 'degenerated into a scandalous exploitation (of patriotism)'; in Madrid, in 1820, a Moderate called them 'grotesque exhibitions ... of the scum of the galleys'.[5]

As the crises mounted, the official street parties became more frequent and they contrasted poignantly with the ruthlessness of radical regimes in defending their revolutions. Conscription was imposed with brutal determination, whether in the Rhineland in 1849, or in Spain, in 1823.[6] These efforts did not always produce the necessary results, but they are irrefutable evidence of the energy of radicals, and of their bravery in the face of overwhelming opposition. In all of this, they were inspired by the example of the Terror.

Radicals behaved differently within the framework of a stable parliamentary regime, if it allowed them to participate in it. In Spain, the Progressives had a radical wing and, by the 1850s, they were becoming a popular party, at least in the cities, some of whom were republicans. The radical element of the Progressives centred on lower grade civil servants and junior army officers, who wanted a more democratic system for professional reasons and longed to break the grip of the Moderates on office and patronage. They were in almost eternal opposition, forming ministries only in a crisis. Nevertheless, the Progressives show that radicalism could evolve into a loyal opposition.[7]

Britain provided even more security. Manhood suffrage found spokesmen within the liberal governments of the 1830s such as Brougham, thus binding its more militant elements – chiefly

71

Chartism – closer to the parliamentary system than elsewhere in Europe, although not without tensions, as will be seen.

The search for support: the politics of fraternity

When radicals were not driven underground entirely, they worked consciously to win a large following among those excluded from politics, a characteristic they shared with socialists and many nationalists. Their goal was to convert the popular classes to parliamentary politics.

In common with liberals, most radicals were, by nature, 'urban animals' at the start of the period. When they thought of 'the popular classes', they usually meant urban artisans. The artisans were the rank and file of Jacobinism in the 1790s, at least according to the radicals' interpretation of the French Revolution. By 1814, radicals saw their alliance with the artisans as natural. The revolutions of 1830 in Paris, 1831 in Belgium and those in Venice and Milan in 1848–49 support their view.[8] Cracks in this 'old alliance' appeared, but for much of the period, radicals assumed artisan support.

Where they could, as in Britain, France, Spain and the Netherlands in the 1830s and 1840s, radicals busied themselves with publishing newspapers, holding meetings and organising debating clubs open to a wide membership. Two strands of radicalism emerged in the course of this agitation. The first was still rooted in Jacobinism: it sought to interest the artisans in the issue of manhood suffrage, to impress the political militancy of Paine's *The Rights of Man* on a post-revolutionary generation of artisans. This attitude dominated the secret societies of the 1820s – the *Carbonari*, the *Comuneros* or the *Chevaliers de la Liberté* – and the students who rioted in Paris in 1820. There were differences within this radicalism, of course, but they shared a set of basic assumptions inherited from the French Revolution.[9]

A new emphasis emerged within radicalism, especially, after 1830, which placed more emphasis on reciprocal responsibilities than political rights, in ways meant to sustain the common bond between urban artisans and bourgeois radicals. Fraternity was essential to achieve political liberty, and to sustain it. This was, in great part, a response to the rise of socialism, at times reflecting a desire on the part of radicals to assimilate with it, but at others, a determination to challenge the concept of class consciousness. In terms of radical activity and propaganda, it reinforced the belief in fraternity, the truest expression of generosity of spirit. Many radicals came to see 'fraternity' as the social cement of a democratic society, serving the same role as religion for reactionaries. Open associations – political clubs and mutual aid societies – became central to them, as expressions of fraternity as much as for practical reasons. In Germany, gymnastic societies also filled this role and, in parts of the Rhineland, they became radical bastions.[10]

Radicalism acquired a religious element, stressing Christian universalism and fellowship. The French radical Hyacinthe Besson stressed duty and fraternity in 1832: 'instead of taking the theories of the rights of man as (our) principles ... (we) take as our foundation the doctrine of duty and this duty, revealed by ... Christ, is universal fraternity.'[11] Radicals absorbed Christian symbols and discourse into their propaganda, and by 1848, many of them were genuinely religious. Although anti-clerical, and always opposed to a politically powerful, established Church, radicals sought to rid themselves of the Enlightenment tag of 'Godless rationalism' which was still attached to liberals.

Radical agitation was always an attempt to penetrate popular culture. It began as a mission to impart a political ideology shaped by the bourgeoisie to the masses, but in the Restoration period it became a desire to absorb elements of popular culture into radicalism, to arrive at 'a red folklore', in the words of Maurice Agulhon.[12] Radicals were capable of learning, as well as agitating. This change occurred in an urban context. During the 1848–49 revolutions in Italy, the radical leaders in Venice and Milan armed militias composed of urban artisans, yet refused the support of mass peasant insurrections; the countryside remained dangerous, reactionary and alien to them. The same was true of the Rhineland, where the intense political life of the urban artisans was absent in the countryside.[13]

However, other radicals took up the challenge of winning over the peasantry. The countryside teemed with unrest in the early nineteenth century, especially where peasants owned or leased property, where they disputed common land rights, such as forests or pastures,[14] and where they were subject to market pressures, usually through cottage industry or commercial farming. Winegrowers came into direct conflict with the state over taxes on drink, as in France.[15] Disputes with landlords, municipal councils and employers were rife, and in a few areas, radical lawyers took up these causes, notably in Provence, where the peasantry lived in large villages – *bourges* – with artisans and the lower bourgeoisie. This mixed social environment was fertile ground for 'fraternity'. During the July Monarchy, the peasantry of Provence – once known as reactionary – turned to the radicals, as shown in the elections of 1849. It is still disputed to what degree this alliance was based on the willingness of radicals to involve themselves in peasant issues or the emergence of genuine ideological awareness in the countryside.[16] The alliance was real, nevertheless.

The events of 1848, in France and elsewhere, reveal the extent to which the radicals had lost ground in urban areas; the artisans turned against them, and they against the artisans, over the radicals' continued belief in economic liberalism. The *Canuts* – the silk workers of Lyon behind the revolt – were condemned by the radical *Journal des Débats* as 'The barbarians who menace society ... in the suburbs of our manufacturing cities'.[17] The rise of independent associations of artisans, more concerned with economic issues than politics, threw some radicals back on their liberal roots and respect for property. At the height of the Spanish revolution of 1843, radicals in the Democratic Party simultaneously incited urban crowds against the Church, and avoided any deviation from economic liberalism, to retain Progressive support. As a result, popular backing for them receded, and they fell back on more reliable, middle-class sources of support, usually army officers and students. All this points towards the wisdom of those radicals who turned to the countryside, in search of allies. Radicalism was fading as a force in urban popular politics, but its traditional combination of economic liberalism and individualistic belief in liberty, appealed to landholding peasants.

When they took up local causes, radicals were drawn away from a belief in rigid centralisation of government. The Spanish *Comuneros*, as their name indicates, favoured municipal self-government and locally controlled people's militias. These aims were put forward in 1820, and finally achieved in the Constitution of 1837. In Hesse-Cassel, in central Germany, radical agitators won considerable levels of support among the peasantry when they organised a series of petition campaigns in the 1820s requesting local self-government, a peasant demand, as well as the granting of a constitution.[18] Radical goals could be swamped by popular issues, in the quest for support, but examples of this kind also show radicals – so often the victims of authority – becoming aware of the need to curb the state in the interests of liberty. This also concerned J. S. Mill, in Britain, but it was rare to find liberals with such views. Tocqueville was a lone voice under the July Monarchy, in his advocacy of local self-government.[19] Radicals relearned the vibrancy of local politics, whereas liberals continued to fear them, as a springboard for reaction.

Radicalism achieved enormous complexity and vitality when it was allowed into the open, even when its Jacobin, republican or nationalist connotations kept out of the political mainstream. Britain after 1832 saw radicalism flourish in the Chartist movement and the writings of J. S. Mill. In Britain, radicals felt freer to develop philosophic arguments than elsewhere. Mill and Cobbett separated the reforms of the French Revolution from its events, thus allowing manhood suffrage to be debated by those in power, even if they rejected it.[20] A section of English radicalism became respectable and entered the political mainstream; there were openly radical MPs. However, more militant radicals – in England and elsewhere – pointed out that it was wholly unsuccessful in achieving its major goal. Judged by the essential standard of gaining manhood suffrage, Brougham, in Parliament, and the Chartists, on the streets in the 1840s, failed more abjectly than the revolutionaries in France or Germany.

To the true militant, English radicalism represented failure, not success: radicalism could enter the mainstream only by emasculating itself. An older, fiercer tradition survived beneath the surface of Restoration politics.

The professional revolutionary: the politics of militancy

Radicals always lived on a knife's edge. They were seldom allowed into the mainstream of politics and even when they were, their welcome was rarely assured. They were virtual outlaws in most of the German and Italian states, and their taste for republicanism made them suspect in France and Spain.

In France, they were allowed considerable scope in the first years of the July Monarchy, as a reward for their prominent part in the revolution. However, frightened by disturbances in Paris and the serious artisan revolt in Lyon in 1834, tighter controls on the press and association effectively drove many radicals underground. Ironically, the Lyon revolt had not been their work but that of the silk workers. These distinctions on the left were lost on a liberal government, more concerned with demonstrations of republicanism. Spanish radicals fared better in the 1830s and 1840s – indeed, a coalition of Moderates and Progressives saved them, along with themselves, from the repressive rule of Espartero, in the revolution of 1843. A Democratic Party emerged in the 1840s, although it was racked by internal divisions and rightly suspected of republicanism and revolutionary activities. This taste for revolution gave the Moderates the excuse they needed to preach a return to order.

Radicals were often driven underground against their will, but the Spanish Democrats displayed a natural unwillingness to abandon the politics of sects and conspiracies that betrayed a contempt for conventional politics. The repression endured by radicals since 1814 – and before – created the 'professional revolutionary', as fundamental a contribution to European political culture as any other in this period. The radicals invented this figure, and passed it on to nationalists and socialists by 1848.

Auguste Blanqui is the paradigm of the professional, radical revolutionary, in his ideas as well as his actions, perhaps all the more so because he liked to call himself a communist. Blanqui was thoroughly middle class – his older brother was a successful academic under the Bourbons – and his 'communism' was based on a voluntary, collective ownership of property. More important to him, was the role of education in society; his belief that ignorance was the only source of poverty was not alien to the views of Spanish Moderates. Blanqui's unswerving belief in the Parisian artisans as the source of republican values, set beside his preference for using the Breton peasant as an illustration of ignorant brutality, placed him instinctively within the tradition of urban radicalism. He was an atheist, a violent nationalist who believed France had a special role to liberate Germany and Britain. Above all, he was a street fighter. In common with the Spanish and Neapolitan rebels of 1820, Blanqui and those like him were the first to the barricades in 1830, 1834 and 1848. The Terror proved that violence was more than a means to an end; it brought about social change. The Republic – fraternity – was forged on the barricades and the true test of generosity was physical courage. Between revolutions – which radicals of his stamp could only join, not create – he busied himself with plots to launch them, such as his farcical attempt to raise Paris in 1839, when he betrayed his own definition of courage.[21] Blanqui represents the most active, but also the most futile strand of radicalism. The developments that enriched it and strengthened its appeal – agitating the peasantry, adopting Christianity, supporting decentralisation – passed him by.

Blanqui was not alone. Chartism developed a consciously Jacobin wing in the 1830s, centred on Brontree O'Brien, whose admiration for Jacobinism was even more explicit than that of Blanqui. In 1838, on the eve of a Chartist petition to Parliament, one of O'Brien's supporters, Harney, told a rally in Norwich that '... if their present peaceable petition failed, if the National Petition should be trampled upon, then he should ask them ... for a 10th of August, against the present abominable system.'[22] London radicals remained faithful to an earlier Jacobinism, and its taste for plots. In the provinces, radical militancy of a different kind, influenced by Nonconformist religion, reached back to an indigenous revolutionary tradition, which would be absorbed into socialism.

Radicalism and its times

Radicals sought to ally with the new forces of socialism and nationalism, and to accommodate themselves to liberalism, as the opportunity arose. In the end, they were absorbed or made redundant by these forces, however. They interpreted social and economic change, parliamentary politics and social relationships in terms of a single political issue, manhood suffrage. Radicals hoped that if this goal was achieved, their material world would remain intact, even if the moral and social environment would be changed for the best. For all their endeavour, radicals were firmly rooted in their own times, and finally, were left behind. They inspired revolutions, but did not spark them; organised resistance, but did not profit from victory. Their reputations frightened those in authority; in France and parts of Germany and Italy, they saw their dreams realised in 1848, but it did not profit them. Radicalism did not survive the Restoration period. Socialism and nationalism took its place, even for many radicals.

Notes

1 Cited in M. David, *Le Printemps de la Fraternité. Genèse et vicissitudes, 1830-1851*, Paris, 1992, p. 181.

2 Cited in Comellas, *El Trieno*, p. 23.

3 M. Agulhon, *The Republican Experiment, 1848-1852*, Eng. trans. Cambridge, 1982; J. Sperber, *Rhineland Radicals*, Princeton, 1991, pp. 431-7.

4 Cited in G. Spini, *Mito e Realtà della Spagna nelle Rivoluzioni Italiane del 1820-21*, Rome, 1950, p. 81.

5 David, *Le Printemps*, p. 184; Comellas, *El Trieno*, p. 27.

6 Sperber, *Rhineland*, pp. 428-31. Comellas, *Trieno*, pp. 371-5.

7 E. Pidal-Menendez *Historia de España*, vol. 34, Madrid, 1981, pp. 419-21.

8 D. H. Pinkney, *The French Revolution of 1830*, Princeton, 1972, 'The crowd in the French Revolution of 1830', in J. Merriman, ed., *1830 in France*, New York, 1976. On Belgium: C. H. Church, *Europe in 1830. Revolution and Political Change*, London, 1983, pp. 79-94. On Venice: Ginsborg, *Manin*. On Milan: F. Della Peruta, 'Le campagne lombarde nel Risorgimento', *Democrazia e socialismo nel Risorgimento*, Rome, 1965.

9 In a French context: A. Spitzer, *The French Generation of 1820*, Princeton, 1987; A. Spitzer, *Old Hatreds and Young Hopes*, Cambridge, Mass., 1971.

10 Sperber, *Rhineland*, pp. 95-7.

11 Cited in David, *Le Printemps*, p. 62.

12 M. Agulhon, *La République au Village*, Paris, 1979, p. 266.

13 Della Peruta, *Democrazia*; P. Ginsborg, 'Peasants and revolutionaries in Venice and the Veneto, 1848', *Historical Journal*, 17, 1974; Sperber, *Rhineland*, p. 135.

14 P. Sahlins, *Forest Rites. The War of the Demoiselles in Nineteenth-Century France*, Cambridge, Mass., 1994; J. Merriman,'The Demoiselles of the Ariège, 1829-31', in *France in 1830*.

15 R. Price, 'Popular disturbances in the French provinces after the July Revolution', *European Studies Review*, 1, 1971, pp. 323-50.

16 Among those disputing the political awareness of the peasantry: E. Weber, *Peasants into Frenchmen*, Stanford, 1977; T. Judt, *Socialism in Provence*, London, 1981.

17 Cited in Collingham, *July Monarchy*, p. 64. See also, R. Bezucha, *The Lyon Uprising of 1834*, Cambridge, Mass., 1974.

18 K. H. Werget, 'Restoration radicals and "organic liberalism": Einheit-Freiheit reconsidered', *Canadian Journal of History*, 12, 1978, pp. 299-323.

19 F. Mélonio, *Tocqueville et les français*, Paris, 1993, pp. 204-13.

20 J. Dinwiddy, 'English radicals and the French Revolution, 1800-

1850', in Furet and Ozouf, *Political Culture*, pp. 447-66.

21 A. Spitzer, *The Revolutionary Theories of Louis-Auguste Blanqui*, New York, 1957.

22 Cited in Dinwiddy, 'English Radicals', p. 459. 10th August, 1792 was the day Louis XVI was overthrown and the Republic proclaimed.

6

Socialism:
the ideology of change

The varieties of socialism

Socialism entered the political terminology of Restoration Europe less as a declaration of partisan loyalty, than as an expression of interest in the changing conditions of society. Initially, to be socialist was to care about 'the social question', the material conditions of the popular classes. Almost inevitably, those who took such an interest – or expressed it in these terms – were 'of the Left', hence socialism's association with radicalism in its early phases.

The meaning of socialism was in flux before 1848, but, increasingly, socialists became aware of what they were not. In general terms, socialists defined themselves as those who put the 'social question' before all else; they believed that the material condition of the masses was the greatest question of the age. This divided them from the radicals, at the level of theory. When the prospect of power was distant for radicals and socialists – as it was most of the time – this could matter very little, if at all, and so it was possible for them to work together. However, in those brief moments of crisis, these differences became crucial. Socialists saw the great radical demand, manhood suffrage, as at best a means to an end, not as an end in itself. The merest sniff of success on the barricades could bring this divergence into the open.

This does not mean there were no differences among socialists. Their position on the margins of politics – and often of the law – meant that socialist thinkers enjoyed enormous independence. The result was almost as many theories as there were socialists. Three major strands of socialist thought emerged, nevertheless. The first arose from radicalism, within the artisan classes; it looked back to the traditions of popular protest of the French Revolution and beyond and centred on specific economic demands, usually

80

linked to the political programme of the radicals. This has been called 'Jacobin socialism' and it drew on the corporate traditions of the trade guilds, public petitions and, above all, the insurrectionary tradition of the French Revolution. It was archaic, lacking in sophisticated theory or coherence and backward looking. Pierre-Joseph Proudhon was the thinker who reflected its views most closely, but Jacobin socialism was about action, not debate. This form of socialism was rooted entirely in its own times, and condemned by other socialists, especially Marx, for being so. However, it was among the largest, most widespread and genuinely popular movements of the early nineteenth century. It shared these features with reaction, together with the fact that it was doomed.

The second form of socialism to emerge before 1848 is referred to as 'Utopian socialism'. It was not a popular movement in origin, but it often attained a popular following because it addressed – and sought to redress – the problems of the artisan classes. Among its major figures were Charles Fourier and Etienne Cabet, in France, and Robert Owen, in Britain. As their name suggests, 'Utopians' turned their backs on politics, concentrating their efforts on creating model communities, or theories of how best to organise them. Where they found a following, it was because their ideas were inspired by contemporary needs. Whereas 'Jacobin socialism' was the socialism of the artisans, 'Utopian socialism' was socialism for the artisans.

'Scientific socialism' was one of the few ideologies of the early nineteenth century that looked forward, without concessions to the present. As a result, it remained unpopular and impotent in its own times, but made a fundamental impact on the future. Its two major wings were the St Simonians, in France, and Karl Marx. For all their differences, Marx and the St Simonians shared an impatience with their own times, which they regarded as nothing more than a period of transition towards an urbanised, society and an industrial economy. Their thoughts centred on the rise of a powerful state, fuelled by modern technology, and the emergence of new socio-economic classes: a capitalist bourgeoisie that derived its wealth from industry, not agriculture or the professions and an industrial proletariat which would displace the artisans, before it swept away the bourgeoisie. They had little time for contemporary grievances, save as a way of stirring revolution. If 'Jacobin socialism' was the brand of socialism those in power feared most, 'scientific socialism' was that which conservatives, especially, came most to respect, particularly when it won a certain following through trade unions, the form of organisation it regarded as appropriate to new conditions. Bismarck took seriously the German neo-Marxist and union leader, Lassalle; Napoleon III respected the St Simonians and brought them into his governments. They were united by a growing contempt for the inadequate responses of liberalism and radicalism to the winds of economic change. 'Jacobin socialists' were driven by a contempt for all those in power – liberal or conservative – and by many radicals who aspired to it, to engage with contemporary problems.

'Jacobin socialism': the 'social question' and the break with radicalism

The alliance between radicals and urban artisans owed more to their shared memory of the French Revolution, than to contemporary realities. Even at the height of the Terror period, Robespierre gave way to demands for price-fixing of basic commodities with reluctance. The partnership was real enough in practice, until the 1830s, but it was based on a mutual illusion.

The most important result of the French Revolution for the artisans – inside France and wherever French reforms were adopted – was the abolition of the guilds and the ending of restrictions on trade and profession. This freeing of the market affected artisans far more than the pangs of industrialisation. The factory system was not yet widespread in most of Europe, outside Britain, and, although new machinery frightened the artisans, their real problems were stagnant wages, overcrowded trades and, above all, the 'unfair' competition which followed the end of guild control of standards and membership. Artisans could now undercut each other or, more usually, be undercut by bourgeois entrepreneurs who employed cheaper labour than trained craftsmen. Thus, western Europe teemed with labour disputes between 1814 and 1848. For instance, in the Düsseldorf area alone, there were between two thousand and three thousand disputes of this type every year in the 1840s.[1] This was the breeding ground of 'Jacobin socialism'.

Radicals perceived these conflicts as setting the artisan against the state; in fact, they pitted the artisans against liberalism, root and branch. Radicals could exploit them, but they could depend on the artisans only if they, themselves, abandoned economic liberalism. Few did so. In defiance of liberal individualism, many groups of artisans revived certain aspects of the guilds on the margins of the law, either through mutual aid societies – which were legal – or more clandestine associations, which maintained informal rules akin to those of the guilds. In France, they were called *compagnonnages*, while in many German states, the guilds still existed, but their legal authority had been undercut or removed. This was where artisan political culture developed, well out of the reach of most radicals. Its demands surfaced in the revolutions of 1830 and 1848, when artisans petitioned the new liberal regimes in vain, to restrain or revoke liberty of profession, to allow freedom of association for the crafts and sometimes to ban the new technology of mass production. Manhood suffrage was worthless to them, if it could not deliver these demands. As things stood, the liberal governments they had to deal with rejected their demands out of hand. They also condemned their methods of peaceful protest, petitioning, as an illegal, collectivist form of association, thus underlining the gap between liberal ideology and artisan aspirations.

The risings the artisans made by and for themselves reveal the growing split with radicalism, as has already been seen in Lyon in 1834, when many radicals condemned the silk workers. Yet, of even more significance, is that the *canuts* did not look to middle-class radicals for support or direction, as they had in 1830: the rejection was mutual. The rebels produced no political programme, exposing the great weakness of 'Jacobin socialism', but they had lost faith in the radicals. Barcelona in the 1840s and early 1850s, shows how workers could invert their traditional dependence on radicals, through new forms of organisation, however. When the liberal regime banned guild-type associations in 1838, a 'Workers' Mutual Protection Society' was formed, which developed into the most mature body of its kind in Europe, although it existed only in a small area around the city. The strong guild traditions of Barcelona gave it life, but it did not look back. Its methods of organisation fostered political awareness among the 50,000 members it had by 1843. Its local sections worked for practical ends – wages, conditions and welfare – but did so through popularly elected delegates to a central committee. Its great leaders were Juan Muns and Clavé, who were workers themselves. The union survived repression in the 1840s, to re-emerge after 1850 in a position of strength. By the 1850s, radical republicans were courting its support.[2] Barcelona is a unique case, but it reveals that radicalism could be done without, if artisans were prepared to adapt.

If 'Jacobin socialism' had a theorist, it was Pierre-Joseph Proudhon, a self-educated French printer. In common with reactionary thinkers, Proudhon believed that the 'evil of the age' was the separation of ethics from politics and economics. He also questioned whether the abstract doctrines of economic liberals reflected reality. Proudhon turned, instead, to formulating a rigid code of 'justice' for everyday conduct. Not withstanding his famous slogan, 'property is theft', Proudhon's concept of 'justice' entailed the defence of modest private property, but demanded the regulation of the way property owners behaved. Private ownership had to be 'purified'; what had to be eliminated was 'the sum total of abuses inherent in the institution of private ownership'[3] – the ability of property owners to exploit the landless. Proudhon actually sought to protect small business and farms through a system of credit banks. This set him beyond the pale of socialism as it later developed, but it rooted Proudhon firmly in his own times, in his fear of the state and the belief that property was the only guarantee of independence from it. For all its idiosyncrasies, Proudhon's ideas offered a political future to radicals, especially because they embraced the peasantry. An artisan himself, Proudhon saw through the radicals in 1848, and did not support them.

Utopian socialism: a modern dream

Charles Fourier and Etienne Cabet were radical republicans who turned their backs on the politics of revolution and conspiracy, although they retained strong roots in the Jacobin tradition. Cabet, like Mazzini and Blanqui, was a disillusioned *Carbonaro*. Like them, and in common with Proudhon and many reactionaries, these Utopians feared for a society that seemed to have dissolved into egotistical, selfish chaos. They sought consciously to form a bridge between the need to redress the material grievances of the masses and the spiritual void they perceived at the heart of society. Neither the political reforms of the radicals, nor the 'scientific' projects of Marxists and St Simonians were enough on their own, to redress the 'social question'. Indeed, these thinkers mark an important stage in the rejection of the political culture of the Restoration period, and the emergence of new ideologies.

Utopians made a deliberate effort to shift the path of reform away from conventional politics, in other directions. In so doing, they were able to free themselves from the traditions of 'Jacobin socialism' and concentrate on the elements of change in the early nineteenth century. In common with 'scientific socialists', they emphasised the importance of the new elements in the European economy – urbanisation, industrialisation and the replacement of the artisan and peasant classes with a propertyless proletariat. It was simply assumed by most Utopians that the future of society lay in this direction, and that existing political ideologies would become redundant, along with the classes and interests they served. In many ways, the Utopians were right; they were astute critics of their own times.

They certainly touched a nerve in sections of the urban working classes, for their writings were very popular, and some Utopian ideas found their way into the thinking of the workers' associations. Much of this appeal was in the sillier, more emotional aspects of their thought. However absurd, their obsession with 'fraternity' and 'brotherhood' offered the promise of humanity in a splintered society. Cabet wrote his widely read *Voyage en Icarie* in 1842. It was a 'novel' about Icaria, a mythical land which provided the model of a just society, hence why his followers were called Icarians. The form, itself, indicates his ability to reach a wide audience, in a new way. Cabet's society was unlike that advocated by Proudhon; it had nothing to do with the specific aspirations of the artisans. Icaria was a communist society, where the democratic, centralised state is the only property owner, and where labour is done by the new technology, insofar as his imagination could conceive it. More emphatically than any radical had ever done, Cabet placed equality above liberty, and offered a vision of material well-being and security – infused with a gentle, neo-Christian pacifism – in place of the 'sound and fury' of the revolutionary tradition of radicalism. Cabet stood out, in this period, in his belief in non-violence. His ideas offered a welcome vision during the 'hungry forties'. As Maurice Agulhon has said of the workers of the naval shipyards of the French port of Toulon, the *Voyage* was by the side of the workers, as if it were a part of the workers' movement, in itself.[4] The events of 1848 destroyed Cabet's last hopes for the realisation of his ideas in Europe. He left for America, to form a model community – Icaria – in the mid-west, which failed.

Fourier began from the proposition that the doctrines of economic liberalism were the 'poisoned fruit' of the French Revolution. He agreed with Cabet – and the 'scientific socialists' – that industrialisation was inevitable, and he emphasised, even more than Cabet, that it had to be made palatable. However, this desire to 'soften the blow' stemmed from a conviction that the whole process was unnatural. Insofar as possible the new society was to resemble the lost, pre-industrial rural world. Although communitarian, society would revolve around small, independent villages, *phalansteries*. Work would include traditional agrarian tasks. The ultimate aim was self sufficiency, and Fourier remained deeply suspicious of technology – and hostile to urbanisation – in his vision of the future. Fourier probably appealed more to the isolated, submerged lower middle classes than to the urban workers, and he showed a compassion for social outcasts usually lacking in the tightly-knit milieu of 'Jacobin socialists'. Almost alone among Restoration reformers, Fourier was a feminist. Whereas almost every other political thinker of the period took conflict for granted, Fourier thought it was unnecessary and believed social change would arise from an end to emotional and social repression.

Scientific socialism: a blueprint for change

'Scientific socialism' had much in common with Utopianism, in that it looked to the new developments in technology and the economy as keys to the future of Europe, rather than to a defence of social classes as they existed in the early nineteenth century. The two main exponents of 'scientific socialism' were Marx, Engels and a looser group called the St Simonians. They held themselves aloof from the struggles of the artisans, or, in the case of Marx, tried to infiltrate them only out of expediency, as during the revolutions of 1848, when Marx virtually admitted that the only way to bring about a revolution in Germany was to tag his Communist League onto the more widespread 'Jacobin' activities of the radicals. Both Marx and Engels admitted their movement lacked 'the common touch'.[5]

When it was a matter of confronting the hard realities of contemporary politics, especially as thrown up by revolution, Marx displayed a consistent ability to get things wrong. After the 'June Days' in Paris, in 1848, he produced *The Class Struggle in France*, where he saw what he wanted to see: a revolt not of the artisan classes, but of the new, industrial proletariate. He was wrong, of course, and the account he wrote later, *The Eighteen Brumaire of Louis Napoleon Bonaparte*, is in some ways a retraction of his earlier assessment, and also a perceptive study of why socialism did not become a crucial factor in 1848. Marx himself soon saw that nothing could be achieved without a large alliance of radicals and socialists and, after 1848, he doubted even this. Instead, he looked to longer term, structural changes in society that would make contemporary issues redundant in the near future. Hence, in 1846, Marx and his followers were openly contemptuous of the views of Wilhelm Weitling, the leading spokesman of Christian, Utopian socialism, whose priority was to alleviate the distress of the artisan class to which he belonged.

Yet it was precisely because 'scientific socialism' was so concerned with future trends that it lost its way so utterly when meddling in contemporary affairs. Marxist theory was preoccupied with the rise of new classes – a capitalist bourgeoisie and an industrial proletariate – fighting for power in a new, urban environment. This was not a matter for regret, simply part of a wider process of history, thus Marxist socialism carried none of the sentimental, emotional baggage of Utopianism – and none of its popular following, either. Liberalism would triumph in the middle term, but would prove unable to master the new forces at work in society; a new, collectivist order would emerge, dominated by the proletariat, the largest group in society.

The St Simomians took a similar attitude to the present, if not to the future. This group of French thinkers drew on the esoteric writings of a French aristocrat, Henri de St Simon, who had a view of contemporary society not unlike that of Marx. He divided it into the 'idle classes' on the one hand – those doomed to disappear, like the artisans and those already redundant, like the landed nobility

– and the 'industrial classes' on the other, the new industrial proletariat and the capitalist bourgeoisie. Unlike Marx, St Simon and
his followers did not see the new classes in conflict with each
other, but in partnership, as long as society remained fluid and
open to what would now be termed 'upward mobility'. Also unlike Marx, the St Simomians had a Utopian element within them,
believing in the need for a 'church' of sorts, and often subscribing
to lunatic notions of private morality, akin to Fourier's.

This combination of licentiousness and elitism denied them a
popular following, but their belief in technology as the key to
progress, together with their acute analyses of the new factors at
work in society, led many St Simonians closer to the centre of
power than any other branch of socialism. In common with conservative reformers – and unlike most contemporary political
thinkers – St Simonians such as Michel Chevalier, Prosper
Enfantin and the Péreires brothers, perceived the potential power
of the state, and made it the centre of their vision of the future.
Banking, industry and production needed to be co-ordinated by a
modern, professional state, for the benefits of capitalism to be enjoyed by all. They integrated easily into the regime of Napoleon
III, after the revolutions of 1848, where their more practical ideas
had a considerable influence on government policy. As its mystical, quasi-religious elements fell away, the St Simonians emerged
as the strongest force in contemporary socialist thought.

St Simonianism represented an attempt to 'humanise' the new
social order. Even more than Fourier, its adherents were committed to sexual equality – as well as to promiscuity. Enfantin declared that 'What moved me even more than the wretchedness of
the people was the fraudulent ... relations between men and
women'.[6] Their behaviour may have been puerile in such matters,
but their perceptions are still relevant. The St Simonians had a tre-
mendous influence after 1848, but even beyond this, perhaps more
than any other thinkers of the nineteenth century, they have the
right to be seen as ahead of their times.

Socialism in politics

The impact of socialist thinkers on the politics of the period was
minimal; even the St Simomians did not take their place in the sun
until after 1851. The most politically successful socialist was Louis

Blanc, a French journalist, who combined traditional radicalism –
especially a belief in manhood suffrage – with sharp criticisms of
'the cowardly and brutal principle of competition', as practised
under the July Monarchy, as he put it in his widely read book *The
Organisation of Labour.*[7] Blanc was eloquent and tireless in his
efforts before 1848, and he became a member of the executive of
the Provisional government during the revolution. Blanc fought
for the 'right to work', and chaired the Luxembourg Commission
which set up the National Workshops as opening the way to a
more benevolent, socialist state. The Commission fell prey, instead, to the older rivalries of the guilds, then to liberal misgivings
about government intervention in the economy. Blanc was swept
from office after the 'June Days', his vision repudiated by liberal
deputies and the rebellious artisans, alike. Proudhon was correct
in his assessment that Blanc was naive to hope that so interven-
tionist a scheme would be supported by the Provisional Government.

Blanc's tenure of office ended in failure, and it illustrates the
impossibility of reconciling socialism with any political system
which accepted liberal economics as its foundation. This was why
socialism was most influential – however indirectly – in states
dominated by conservative reformers, most notably Prussia.

During the 1840s, and especially after the revolt of the Silesian
weavers in 1844, the minds of many in the Prussian government
had been concentrated on the problem of urban poverty, and the
regime showed itself ready to adopt welfare legislation of an advanced kind, a policy of 'social conservatism'. The major social
legislation followed the 1848 revolution, but the Prussian monarchy already showed itself more aware of these problems – and
more willing to use the state to solve them – than truly liberal regimes. The influence of socialist thinkers was acquired at several
removes – usually through reactionary ideologues, particularly
Hermann Wagener, who was later instrumental in bringing together Bismarck and Lassalle, the labour leader.

By 1848, it was increasingly evident that 'Jacobin socialism'
would soon become a thing of the past, but it was not yet clear that
'scientific socialism' had charted the contours of the future. Only
with the passing of the artisans and the rise of industrial trade unions, would socialism usurp radicalism.

Notes

1 Speber, *Rhineland*, p. 56.
2 *Historia de España*, VII, pp. 773-82.
3 Cited in G. Litcheim, *The Origins of Socialism*, New York, 1969, p. 90.
4 M. Agulhon, *Une Ville Ouvrière au Temps du Socialisme Utopique. Toulon, 1815 à 1851*, Paris, 1970, p. 264.
5 Sperber, *Rhineland*, pp. 297-304.
6 Cited in F. E. Manuel, *The Prophets of Paris*, Cambridge, Mass., 1962, p. 188.
7 Cited in Sewell, *Work and Revolution*, p. 233.

Nationalism:
the ideology of unity

The importance of nationalism as a political force has been greatly exaggerated for the years 1814-51. In common with radicalism, socialism and reaction, it lived on the margins of mainstream politics. Nevertheless, these decades were a formative period for its development. As with so many aspects of the political culture of the Restoration period, the concept of nationalism is all the more deceptive to the modern observer, because it seems familiar, but in fact nationalism existed in a very different context from its current form.

Benedict Anderson pioneered the concept of 'imagined communities' as the essential basis for a viable, popular sense of national identity. That is, it is impossible for all members of a nation-state to know each other personally, and this void is filled by a shared culture, common political interests and, above all, a general acceptance of the nation-state as the fundamental social, economic and political unit of human organisation.[1]

The conditions necessary for this sense of shared identity to prevail over wide areas and large populations did not exist in most parts of Europe before the 1840s, when the major impact of changes in communications and urbanisation at last began to be felt. Most of the people of Europe were peasants, living in small, relatively isolated communities; their most important preoccupations derived from these circumstances. Only in what Hugh Seton-Watson has termed 'the old nations' - Britain, France, Spain, Portugal, and Russia[2] - had a sense of national identity based upon language and culture taken root at the heart of the state, guiding many of its key assumptions and, more importantly, those of the mass of its subjects. As will be seen, even in these cases, a clear concept of shared national identity could not always be taken for granted. Even where a national identity was perceived in these communities, it need not be the most important factor in their political life.

In these circumstances, nationalism could never achieve the mass following craved by its thinkers. It was a weak political creed, incapable of standing by itself in these years. Nationalism 'fed' off other ideologies: it took its model of the state from liberalism; it drew on democracy, as advocated by radicals, for its ideas on political organisation; it achieved a popular following only when and where it adopted elements of reaction, notably religious connotations. Nationalists could hope to enter mainstream politics, only in conjunction with these other elements. When its supporters tried to subordinate liberal, radical or reactionary preoccupations to their own, they quickly found themselves in the wilderness. John Breuilly has discerned this trend in the failure of Mazzini to influence radicals and liberals during the 1848-49 revolutions in northern Italy. He states, 'precisely because his pure nationalism had no diplomatic, dynastic, liberal or popular appeal it could not become the central element within a significant political movement.'[3] It is well worth noting, that nationalist movements outside the 'old nations' achieved a degree of success only when they allied with liberal regimes between 1830 and 1848; they reached their zenith - and their goals - only when they collaborated with conservative regimes, after the revolutions of 1848-49.

Objective reality and subjective perceptions are never synonymous in any period of history; even the most astute politicians do not always read the signs of the times correctly. This was as true of the Restoration as any other era, and part of the reason for the exaggerated role given to nationalism before 1848 lies with Metternich and other conservative leaders. The Habsburg monarchy and its servants were particularly aware of the damage nationalism could do to their state, if it became a popular movement: it would destroy it. However, Metternich - and Francis II, on his advice - often mistook the potential for the reality. They developed a fear of nationalist agitation out of all proportion to its true strength, or, more correctly, to its weakness. Indeed, this mistaken panic induced among them by the activities of isolated intellectuals - which lay behind the Carlsbad decrees of 1819 and the massive expenditures on the secret police of the Italian states - is underlined by the success of Metternich's own approach to nationalism in Germany and Italy. Metternich opposed the would-be populist nationalism of his opponents by encouraging the individual states of Italy and the German Confederation to work together, to keep other powers - notably France and Russia - from interfering in their affairs. He perceived a common interest among the states of these regions.[4] So often derided as a retrograde figure, Metternich's greatest failing was, in fact, succumbing to pessimism about the ability of the forces of nationalism and socialism to undermine his projects. He was ahead of his times, not behind them.

Nevertheless, the origins of Metternich's fears derived from the powerful combination of radicalism and nationalism achieved and released by Revolutionary France. His fear - and the hope of many French radicals - was that it could be revived. To this, he might have added the powerful nationalisms awakened in Britain and Russia, in the course of the Napoleonic wars. Nationalism was most potent in the 'old nations'. They might serve as examples of its real power, as opposed to its potential.

State nationalism – the politics of unity

Of all the European states, Great Britain possessed more of the preconditions for the emergence of an 'imagined community' than any other, and there is considerable evidence to support the case made recently by Linda Colley that such a community had come into being, and that the ruling elite was deeply conscious of its existence.[5] Britain was relatively small, possessed of good communications and of a reasonably numerous educated class. The religious unity achieved in the early modern period was reinforced strongly during the long wars of the eighteenth century against France - the leading Catholic power until the Revolution. Leaving aside earlier signs of national awakening, which date as far back as Shakespeare and even possibly Chaucer, the wars of the eighteenth century forged a widespread sense of commitment to the British state among the popular classes, which overrode local or regional differences. Most Britons continued to live in relatively small, inward-looking rural communities, but the prolonged war effort encouraged them to look to the centre - to the Monarchy, the established Church of England and to Parliament - if seldom to the neighbouring county.

The last phases of the Napoleonic wars saw the mobilisation of unprecedented numbers of men; in this way, almost every part of the country, and all social classes, were drawn into a common cause. This was equally true of all the Great Powers, but in Britain, the state was able to draw upon a powerful national myth based on a widely shared vision of Britain as a bastion of relative freedom - a freedom inextricably linked to Protestantism - assailed by an authoritarian, economically retrograde France. The end of the wars saw the source of this common unity dissolve, however. Indeed, the Restoration period was probably the moment in modern times when Britain came closest to lacking any focal point for national unity: France was gone as a source of fear and, in 1829, the confessional unity of the state was breached by the granting of Catholic Emancipation.

The power of British nationalism endured, nevertheless. It is evident less at the level of political theory, than in the behaviour of those involved in politics. The tradition of petitioning Parliament, especially by the radicals, has already been discussed in political terms, but it is an equally important indication of nationalism. Parliament remained a focus of hope for people all over Britain - in Scotland and Wales, as well as England - and, as such, a natural, instinctively acknowledged source of authority. This emerges not just in the concerted, nationwide campaign to pass the First Reform Act, before 1832, but in the fact that those disappointed by the terms of the Act, the Chartists above all, did not break with the concept of a united polity. Instead of rejecting national politics, they continued, in vain, to petition Parliament for manhood suffrage.

In the context of nationalism, is the shared acceptance of the authority of a British state by those inside and outside the political world. Parliament was to be reformed, perhaps even purged, but not replaced. For all its failings, the concept of Britain as a relatively free country, thanks to its parliamentary traditions, survived the disappointments of 1832. The centrality of liberty to British nationalism was also acknowledged by those in power. The abolition of slavery throughout the empire in 1833 allowed the ruling classes to drape themselves in this tradition, not only because of the character of the legislation, but from the fact that it followed a petitioning campaign of enormous proportions.[6] Popular nationalism redefined itself in the first half of the ninteenth century, with a minimum of conscious effort by the state, yet managed to remain centred on the institutions of the state.

Britain and Russia regarded themselves as having nothing in common in the nineteenth century: British nationalism was increasingly founded on the uniqueness of British liberties; Russian nationalism rested on a concept of 'official nationality' laid down by the state. Indeed, its chief historian, Nicholas Riasanovsky, dates it precisely from the Imperial Decree of Nicholas I, on 2 April, 1833.[7] Its foundation was that of complete obediance to the Tsar, himself, which the contemporary historian Pogodin believed to be 'the secret of Russian history'.[8] In political terms, the gap between Britain and Russia could hardly have been wider, but when the individual components of Nicholas's 'official nationality' are examined, they have several themes in common with Britain.

The three corners of 'official nationality' were the monarchy, the Orthodox religion and the more vaguely expressed concept of 'nationality', which increasingly centred on the spread of the Russian language and literature among the aristocracy, in a determined effort to replace French; later, it also became a policy of 'Russification' against the non-Russian peoples of the empire. Beneath the surface, nationalism in Russia, as in Britain, rested on a widely shared acceptance of a political order, based on monarchy and religion. Although officially defined, the policy was rooted in the historical realities of Russian society, and was capable of binding together a vast state, with poor communications.

There was a duality at the heart of this policy, which stressed duty, sacrifice and unquestioning obedience to the state, yet also raised the common people to an almost mystical level of importance.[9] Outside official circles, this found expression in contemporary literature, ranging from the genius of Pushkin's verse to trite popular histories and collections of folklore. Nicholas I and his ministers stressed the institutional aspects of nationalism. Within the universities, 'Panslavism', a cultural interpretation of official policy, emerged in these years. 'Slavophiles' concentrated on peasant life and popular religion; increasingly, they saw these, rather than the state, as the core of national values.[10]

Ironically, this stress on the peasantry and popular culture derived in great part from western models of romantic nationalism. In western, continental Europe, it proved harder to forge instinctive links between the state and popular culture than in Britain or Russia, and it was in these circumstances - in Italy, Germany and, in slightly different circumstances, in France – that nationalist ideology achieved intellectual coherence, but this was also where it had least relevance to contemporary politics.

Romantic nationalism - the politics of culture

As has been seen, Metternich saw the French Revolution as the fount of nationalist ideology, and regarded the concepts of radicalism and nationalism as inextricably interwoven. He was correct, up to a point, in that nationalist ideologues in France, Italy and Germany came to see manhood suffrage as a central component of nationalism, but it was not always essential to them. Indeed, Metternich's vision fails to do justice to the importance of the cultural, as distinct from political, goals of romantic nationalists. Beyond the creation of national borders, their political vision often had less coherence than he gave them credit for.

The reforms of the Revolution had created the best framework in which a nation might develop, but no more: they did not create an 'imagined community'; only a shared cultural identity, fused with the radicals' concept of 'fraternity' could lead to this. This was the next, crucial stage in human development, according to romantic nationalists, for they saw the world as naturally divided into 'nations', cultural entities which were only awaiting a political expression. All other states were the artificial creations of war and diplomacy; only the re-emergence of 'true' nations would assure peace and stability in Europe.

It may seem odd to bracket the case of France, one of the oldest and most coherent states in Europe, with those of Italy and Germany, where the question of national unification was all to nationalists. However, the French ruling classes emerged from the Revolutionary-Napoleonic period with the two contrasting - and violently opposed - concepts of their national identity. The traditional borders of the state was almost the only aspect of national identity to win general acceptance after 1814. It is arguable that all the political quarrels outlined in the preceding chapters turned on a dispute between the Revolution and the counter-revolution, over what it meant to be French.[11] This debate was watched with great interest by nationalist ideologues in Italy and Germany, and in eastern Europe. It became crucial to their own definitions of what made a nation, and of its centrality to political culture.

France offers a unique example of romantic nationalism being able to influence government policy, not only during the Second Republic of 1848-51, but, at times, during the July Monarchy. To contemporaries, it represented a case of 'stage one' being achieved, and of the struggle to realise 'stage two'. Nationalism in France came to centre less on politics than on culture, at least after 1830, when the reactionary concept of French indentity was effectively driven into the political wilderness. As has been seen, however, the Catholic Church remained a powerful influence on French life, as did provincialism. The common cause of liberals and radicals against these forces was conceived in terms of a nationalist crusade to teach Frenchmen their true cultural identity. The Revolution and then, for radicals, the Second Republic had given them their political rights.

French nationalism had no need for a 'war of liberation'. Rather, it expressed itself through the intense interest taken by the July Monarchy and the Second Republic in education, especially in fostering a standard, national language and the acceptance of a shared national history.

These years saw an outpouring of histories of France, and it is possible to distinguish among them, distinctly nationalist historians. Most leading politicians produced histories of the French Revolution in the 1830s and 1840s, written from their respective point of view: the socialist, Louis Blanc stressed the bourgeois nature of the Revolution, and its failure to achieve popular demands; the liberal republican, Thiers, saw in it the seeds of the perfect political system; Taine, the reactionary, writing later than the others, stressed its destructive elements. The most enduring of all these histories, is that of Jules Michelet. His approach to the Revolution - and to the whole of French history - marks him out as a nationalist above all else. Michelet sought to give the French a history of the Revolution capable of healing its wounds; more than this, he sought to recover the past before 1789 in his *History of France*, the last volume of which appeared in 1843. He rejoiced in the diversity of France, but stressed at all times a shared history of struggle against invaders.

Preoccupations with national identity in this period stretched beyond voluminous histories, however. Popular theatre - *vaude-*

97

ville - created the figure of 'Jean Chauvin', the brave, xenophobic, peasant-soldier, a hero of the Napoleonic wars fallen on hard times, but loyal to his country and repository of a peasant wisdom influenced by state education, the Enlightenment and the army. He had little to do with reality, but he symbolised what romantic nationalists wanted the ordinary Frenchman to be.[12]

This image of the ideal Frenchman as a soldier-peasant would have meant little had its influence not reached into the policy of the state, itself. The army or, to be more precise, conscription, became the cornerstone of cultural nationalism for successive French governments from the July Monarchy onwards, even in peacetime. The army was to become a school for the peasantry, where patriotism and a shared sense of culture were to be acquired - the 'melting pot of early nineteenth-century France' as it has recently been described.[13] When raised to the level of government policy, the means of cultural education became brutal, but the ends remained those of the ideal expressed by Michelet: a new, modern nation of enlightened patriots, close to its peasant roots.

French nationalists had the opportunity to translate their ideals into policy; it was left to the politically powerless nationalists to elaborate the pure ideology of romantic nationalism. Indeed, the more powerless they were, the greater theoreticians they became.

The greatest nationalist thinker of the nineteenth cenutry was Giuseppe Mazzini, whose career has already been mentioned in connection with liberalism and radicalism. When he broke with the *Carbonari* in 1831, his new organisation, Young Italy, became the direct model for other nationalists all over Europe. By the 1840s, it was followed by Young Ireland, Young Germany and many others. Mazzini also had many admirers in Britain - especially the radical, J. S. Mill, and Charles Dickens. However, he had no popular support. He could captivate other intellectuals, but never the Italian masses he so desperately sought to 'awaken'. Historians who admire Mazzini often point to the deep influence he had on Italian politicians of the late nineteenth century, notably Crispi, the powerful liberal prime minister of the 1890s.[14] Much of this 'admiration' by later politicians may have been self-serving, but it reveals two important aspects of the place Mazzini holds in the history of the period. His theories were powerful justifications for the regimes of newly united states. Equally, however, they were only of use after the process of unification had been achieved; they had little impact or relevance to European society in the early nineteenth century, when they were conceived. As a theorist, few could surpass Mazzini, however. He was vague, but he excelled even the radicals in eloquence. It is at this level that his contribution to Restoration political culture must be examined.

Mazzini saw the French Revolution as 'the exhaustion of a principle'[15] and of little relevance to the generation of Europeans of the Restoration period; it had been a purely political movement, and so failed to address 'the real, paramount question - the moral and social question.'[16] The moral and social question hinged on every individual finding his place in his own nation, and blending into a national community with his fellows. Mazzini saw nations as created by God, and thus the only valid form of human organisation. Religious sentiment - if not the Catholic Church - was central to Mazzini, in contrast to the *Carbonari* and most French republicans.

Nationalism was a living, active force in daily life and for Mazzini, it provided the 'social cement' so needed by contemporary society. Thus, Mazzinian nationalism set itself against socialism, because of its belief in the importance of class conflict, believing instead, that feelings of 'brotherhood' between fellow nationals would temper the greed, individualism and egotism of capitalism. Social peace would be the first fruit of deeply felt, collective identity. These views were later developed as a powerful weapon against Marxist socialism,[17] but in terms of practical politics, it simply set the new socialist movement against Mazzini.

There is a great deal in his thought to link Mazzini to the radicals, although as has been seen, he was prepared to compromise over manhood suffrage, to achieve unification, if necessary. However, Mazzini's concept of the nation reached far beyond that held by radicals and liberals, which they derived from the French Revolution. The nation was more than a conglomorate of individuals who shared a common government or even a common culture and language, developed over time, which was the view of French nationalists like Michelet. Language was crucial to Mazzini's definition of a people. French nationalists saw language as a tool, as a means to create unity where it had not existed hitherto: Bretons, Basques and most peasants - with their local dialects - would become French as a result of learning French. Mazzini stood this on its head: language was God given; once a nation lost its language, it lost its identity and ceased to be a nation. He took this concept seriously, and scoffed at his would-be admirers, the Young Ireland movement, in their efforts to rekindle the Gaelic language. For Mazzini, Ireland had ceased to be a true nation.[18] Language, more than territory, was the decisive factor for Mazzini. The nation was finite; it was not an open community, but a complete social organism, which could endure even when denied its rightful political existence.

The emphasis Mazzini placed on culture - and on the eternal nature of the nation in history - was shared by German nationalists. Best known among them are probably the Grimm brothers, whose collections of 'fairy tales' represent a crucial contribution to cultural nationalism in the Restoration period. Like Mazzini, scholars like Wilhelm Grimm and August Boeckh were insistent on the central place of language for national identity, but the ideological foundations of German nationalism differed greatly from those of Mazzini. Whereas Mazzini regarded the popular culture of the countryside - in Italy and elsewhere - as corrupted and primitive, Jacob Grimm devoted his life to the collection and preservation of folk tales because he valued them as repositories of inherited, national wisdom. Similarly, the Grimms investigated peasant dialects with academic care, in their search for the origins of the German language and, therefore, of German identity. In contrast, Mazzini wished to instill in the masses a respect for the canons of Italian high culture - Dante, Machiavelli, Boccaccio.

However, the greatest difference between German nationalists and Mazzinians in Italy and elsewhere, was their views on the relationship of nationalism to the state. The historian, Ranke, expressed the sense of Romantic nationalism, shared with Mazzini, when he wrote:

> Our fatherland is with us, in us ... We are rooted in it from the beginning, and we can never emancipate ourselves from it. This mysterious something that animates the lowliest as well as the greatest, this spiritual atmosphere in which we breathe, precedes every constitution.[19]

This underlines the different approach to national identity through the shared experience of territory, of French Revolutionary nationalism. Yet Ranke and many other German nationalists went further. So central was the shared cultural experience of Germans that it had no need for a political expression; Germany did not need a state because its cultural unity was enough.

In practice, this meant that this strand of German nationalism separated itself from the state. Whereas Mazzini planned guerilla wars of liberation to create a new Italian state, an important section of German nationalists divorced politics from nationalism, and pursued it in academic research and cultural activities. When and where politically active nationalist agitation emerged in Germany, it tended to follow French Revolutionary models, rather than those of Mazzini. John Breuilly has noted that the Frankfurt Parliament did not envisage Germany in ethnic or even linguistic terms; the new state they sought to create was a political entity, not the political expression of a cultural identity.[20]

This comparative approach to nationalist ideas in Italy and Germany reveals three contrasting concepts of the relationship between politics and culture, increasingly at odds with each other before 1848. Mazzini saw politics as the expression of cultural identity; those nationalists closer to the French tradition reversed the process, believing that cultural identity developed from politics. German intellectuals elaborated a 'third way', which divorced national identity from politics. None of them made a major, lasting impact on the politics of the period. The truly great, popular nationalist movements of the early nineteenth century belong to Ireland and to eastern Europe.

Popular nationalism – the politics of kinship

Western nationalists shared a common vision of an ideal society based on warrior-peasants, speaking a common language and sharing culture that had endured in spite of political repression, be it from a feudal, pre-revolutionary monarchy or foreign occupation. It remained a dream for them, at times almost a ridiculous parody of reality. However, in Poland, Hungary, Serbia, Greece, and Ireland, popular nationalist movements emerged in the early nineteenth century. They represented both the ideal and the negation of the theories and hopes of western nationalism.

These cases of mass movements, founded on peasant rebellions or, in the case of Ireland, of a widespread campaign of collective, passive resistance, were admired by many western nationalists and won the sympathy of the liberal governments of the 1830s and 1840s. Support for the Greek and Polish rebels was an important

101

source of unity between French radicals and liberals in the 1830s, and again in 1848; the cause of Catholic Emancipation won the sympathy of English radicals and liberals, and helped to sharpen their own views on the nature of the British state; Greek independence was won with the active military support of France and Britain. The more 'acceptable', liberally inclined leaders of these movements were lionised by the liberal regimes of the 'old nations': Louis Kossuth, the leader of the Hungarian revolt of 1848-49, was greeted by cheering crowds all over Britain after his flight into exile; the Belgians asked Daniel O'Connell to become king of the new, liberal state in 1831.

However, a closer examination of these movements reveals that they were fostered by conditions and embodied aspirations, which were anathema to western nationalist thinkers. These mass movements had two key elements in common: they were based on the peasantry and, even where language was clearly an important element in forging a shared identity, it was really formal, Church-centred religion that provided their cohesion. The powerful forces of shared identity so admired by the west evolved in the absence of a strong state in all of these cases. The Serbian, Greek and Hungarian rebellions took place on the fringe of weak empires. The Ottomans had left the Balkan Christians largely to their own devices for several centuries, allowing them to be governed through their own local notables and, above all, by their priests, according to their own languages and customs; while the Habsburgs had never been able to impose their will on the Hungarian Diet. Alexander I had actually encouraged a degree of autonomy in his Polish provinces after 1814; Ireland had lost its own Parliament only in 1801 and British rule there had been notoriously weak ever since.

Thus, these powerful movements arose from communities that had been allowed to go their own ways over a long period. What emerged were movements much closer to the counter-revolution, such as Carlism, than anything advocated by Mazzini. When western liberal nationalists got too close to them, they emerged bitterly disappointed. Lord Byron, the English poet and self-styled soldier of liberty, was disillusioned when he gave his services to the Greek rebels; they were not the 'warrior-peasants', he imagined, descended from classical heroes, but rather 'ignorant' peasants, bandit chiefs and prosperous merchants, usually led and organised by their clergy. He was repelled to find that their most powerful sense of national identity was the Orthodox religion, and that they drew on a popular culture steeped in the resistance of Christian martyrs of the Islamic Ottoman state. The same conditions, broadly speaking, forged Serb resistance to the Ottomans and both rebellions looked primarily to Russia for help, less because they felt the kind of linguistic bond conceived by the Slavophiles, but because Russia was the greatest Orthodox power.

The most illustrative case of all was probably the conflict between Daniel O'Connell and the Young Ireland movement, in the 1840s. O'Connell, himself, was essentially a liberal, deeply opposed to the emphasis on race and exclusivity brandished by the Mazzinian Young Irelanders in their journal, *The Nation*. He disliked what his most recent biographer has called 'extra-rational politics', a good description of Mazzinian concepts of nationalism in practice.[21] There were other, more practical differences between them, however. O'Connell and his greatest supporters, the Catholic bishops, did not need to flaunt their nationalism in Mazzinian terms. They were native Gaelic speakers, although they preferred English and hoped its greater diffusion among the peasantry would better their economic position; they were also solidly Catholic, and conscious of the importance of religion to the peasantry. In contrast, most of the Young Irelanders - Thomas Davis, John Dillon and Charles Gavan Duffy – were urban intellectuals, some of them Protestants. They relegated religion from the sphere of politics, seeking instead an Irish identity based on the Gaelic language and notions of Celtic race. Nothing could have been further from the reality of Irish nationalism which had, through the nationwide 'Repeal Association', helped O'Connell achieve emancipation by 1829, based as it was on a Catholic peasantry, organised by the Church and led by O'Connell, in a peaceful version of the Greek War of Independence.

Wherever these movements succeeded in winning independence or a degree of autonomy, as in Greece and Serbia, attempts were made by the western, liberal powers to establish constitutional regimes and centralised administrations in the new states. However, these frameworks provoked opposition of a reactionary kind, as peasant communities attempted to preserve their autonomy and reject the secular state. In Ireland, even O'Connell could not prevent the drift away from parliamentary politics towards a peasant nationalism, still rooted in Catholicism, but more concerned with land reform and local vendettas than the creation of a liberal state in Ireland.

Only in Poland and Hungary did romantic, intellectual nationalists eventually succeed in breaking into the mainstream of nationalism. The narrow nationalism of the Polish and Magyar nobles was rooted in the defence of privilege, as has been seen, and their peasants were actually turned against them by the Russian and Austrian governments on several occasions in the early nineteenth century. However, by the 1840s, many within the aristocracy adopted liberal ideas about the state, were converted to nationalist ideas on the importance of language and culture and, above all, adopted the cause of land reform for the peasantry. In Poland, romantic nationalists were almost alone in Europe in embracing the Catholic religion of the peasantry and placing it at the centre of national identity.[22] In these circumstances, popular movements, centred on nationalism and not just influenced by it, were able to emerge and, significantly, to survive military defeat. They survived the turmoil of 1848 better than many aspects of the dominant political culture of the Restoration period.

Notes

1   B. Anderson, *Imagined Communities, Reflections on the Origins and Spread of Nationalism*, London, 1983.

2   H. Seton-Watson, *Nations and States. An enquiry into the origins of nations and the politics of nationalism*, London, 1977.

3   J. Breuilly, *Nationalism and the State*, Manchester, 1982 ed., p. 70.

4   On Germany: R. D. Billinger, *Metternich and the German Question. States' Rights and Federal Duties, 1820-34*, Newark, 1991, pp. 171-3.

5   L. Colley, *Britons. Forging the Nation, 1707-1837*, New Haven, 1992.

6   *Ibid.* pp. 350-60.

7   N. Riasanovsky, *Nicholas I and Official Nationality in Russia, 1825-1855*, Berkeley & Los Angeles, 1959, p. 73.

8   Cited in N. Riasanovsky, *A Parting of the Ways. Government and the Educated Public in Russia, 1801-1855*, Oxford, 1976, p. 118.

9   *Ibid.* p. 125.

10   M. B. Petrovich, *The Emergence of Russian Panslavism*, New York, 1956.

11   For a stimulating discussion, see P. Nora, 'Nation', in F. Furet & M. Ozouf, eds. *A Critical Dictionary of the French Revolution*, Eng. trans.

Cambridge, Mass. & London, 1989, pp. 742-53.

   12   G. de Puymège, *Chauvin, le soldat-labourer*, Paris, 1993.

   13   *Ibid.* p. 148.

   14   See especially, the admiring biography by Denis Mack-Smith, *Mazzini*, New Haven & London, 1994.

   15   G. Mazzini, 'Fede e Avvenire', in L. Salvatorelli, ed., *Opere*, Milan, 1967, 2 vols, II, pp. 224-30, 229.

   16   *Ibid.*

   17   A point stressed by Mack-Smith, *Mazzini*, p. 2. Mazzini knew the work of Marx, and was quick to oppose it.

   18   R. D. Edwards, 'The contribution of Young Ireland to the development of the Irish National idea', in S. Pender, ed., *Tórna Féilscríbhinn*, Cork, 1947.

   19   Cited in Sheehan, *German History*, p. 553.

   20   Breuilly, *Nationalism and the State*, p. 74.

   21   Macdonagh, *O'Connell*, p. 310.

   22   See especially A. Walicki, *Philosophy and Romantic Nationalism. The Case of Poland*, Oxford, 1982.

Conclusion: revolutions

The period 1814–50 was studded with short, sharp and usually failed revolutions: those of 1820–23, 1830–31 and 1848–50, together with the great counter-revolution of the period, the Spanish Carlist War of the 1830s. They were very complex affairs and historians neglect them at their peril. While it is not possible to explore all aspects here, they deserve specific analysis for what they reveal of the political ideologies, labels and discourse of the their own times, so much of which has been passed on to modern Europe. It is in them that all the elements of contemporary politics interacted: in the midst of the tension, uncertainty and violence they generated among contemporaries, labels and positions that may have seemed unclear in normal circumstances suddenly came into sharp relief. For those who lived through them, these revolutions were defining moments in political life. Within their brief compass, they encapsulate the essence of politics in the early nineteenth century.

Revolutions sharpen the mind. The revolutions of the period, and even more the fear or prospect of revolution sharpened the minds of contemporaries over the political terminology that later generations of historians have often had so much trouble with. These conflicts thrust revolutionaries into power, however briefly, and forced them to confront very basic issues – the new forms of government to be adopted chief among them. The crises generated by the revolutions were just as much of a test for those in danger of being overthrown. As such, they tested to the limit the potential for division and co-operation between reactionaries and conservative reformers. Paradoxically, the revolutions created a host of prospects and possibilities for liberals, radicals, socialists, and nationalists which could create degrees of unity unthought of when they were outside the corridors of power. The same could be true of conservatives and reactionaries, when it came to the prevention or suppression of these risings. These very specific conditions were crucial in defining the character of contemporary political culture. Yet they also produced a political terminology that would continue to be used, and used ever more widely, in later periods, in utterly changed circumstances and to very different ends.

Co-operation: Left and Right, 1814–48

(i) The diplomacy of ideology

International relations were deeply coloured by contemporary political ideology between 1814 and 1849. Indeed, they may be considered their guiding principle. It is certainly at this level that power blocs emerged which indicate the existence of a 'Right' and 'Left', of co-operation between liberals and radicals on one side and reactionaries and conservatives on the other. There would seem to have been a greater ability to coalesce at the level of diplomacy than at that of domestic politics.

Metternich based much of his strategy to preserve a conservative Europe on stressing the potential – if not always the imminence – of revolution by radical or nationalist elements. This was aimed less at an active repression of subversive forces (except in times of outright crisis), than at keeping reactionary regimes mindful of the need for conservative reform, and consequently, at keeping reactionaries and conservatives from each others' throats. For the forces of the Right, this desired unity usually came after the event, but was stressed by Metternich and his supporters at all times. Nevertheless, when the forces of the Right could act in unison, the results were momentous.

The military activities of the Holy Alliance in Spain and Italy, in the suppression of the revolutions of 1820–23 were the chief manifestation of this. However, these interventions were the work of conservative regimes – Austria and France – in aid of regimes which had lapsed into reaction and, in a sense, were the great 'We told you so' of conservative reformers. In the case of France, the reformers veered towards liberalism, in that of Austria, they looked towards enlightened authoritarianism, but both responded similarly to governments who seemed to have abandoned any commitment to constitutional restraints of any kind. The heat of revolution could distinguish conservative from reactionary, as well as bring them together. The last manifestation of this was the intervention of Russia in Hungary, in 1849, when Nicholas I sent troops to help the Austrians suppress the Hungarian Revolution.

By the early 1830s, an alliance of liberal powers emerged in western Europe, less to challenge the Holy Alliance than to police the continent in the interests of emergent parliamentary regimes, especially in the Iberian peninsula. Perhaps the most spectacular example of all, if not one often assigned the importance it deserves by historians, was the unity among liberals and radicals brought about by the Carlist Wars in Spain in the 1830s. A massive counter-revolution in northern Spain threatened to overturn the thoroughly liberal constitution of 1834. The struggle against Carlism brought not only Spanish liberals and radicals together to a degree unthinkable before, but created something very close to a liberal version of the Holy Alliance in international politics, at whose bidding the French had crushed the revolution of 1820–23. The liberal British government – the first of the post-Reform Act period, the July Monarchy of the 1830 revolution in France under Louis Philippe and the liberal government of Portugal – itself recently rescued from a counter-revolution akin to Carlism – all rallied to the cause of liberal Spain with generous contributions of money and arms for the regime of Maria-Christina, the regent. Both in 1823 and again in 1834, events in Spain showed that contemporary leaders had clear ideas of what constituted acceptable and unacceptable political regimes: in 1823, it was radicalism that was intolerable to the Great Powers. A decade later, reaction had changed places with it, a reflection on the extent to which the political worlds of Britain, France and Spain had also changed in the intervening years.

The earlier revolutions of 1820–23 in Italy and Spain had seen the emergence of similar attitudes in the ranks of the radicals who held power briefly in Madrid, Naples, Palermo, and Turin. The revolutionaries in Italy were explicit about their ideological debt to the Cortez of Cadiz of 1810–13, above all in their adoption of the Spanish Constitution of 1812. This bespoke a shared political tradition that had been forged during the last phases of the Napoleonic Wars, when liberals and radicals alike in southern Italy looked to the Spanish as a mentor. It was a political tradition that was forged in the struggle against the reforming conservatism of the Napoleonic state and was reborn in the later assault on reaction, after the Vienna Settlement. At the height of the struggle there were also considerable hopes that a new 'southern bloc' would emerge to challenge the Holy Alliance, but this should not be confused with the inaccurate contemporary view that the revolutions themselves were the work of an international radical conspiracy. In reality, it was only after the revolutionaries appeared to have got a grip on power that mutual assistance was discussed. When the prospect of Austrian intervention in Naples loomed in the autumn of 1820, the Spanish government tried to mediate on behalf of the Neapolitan rebels; in January, 1821, it made a formal protest against the intervention, its own isolation in Europe not withstanding. These efforts were made by the liberal foreign minister, Perez, in a show of unity with the radicals. However, by April, the radicals were clamouring to form an alliance with Britain, France and Portugal in an effort to save the rebel governments in Naples and Turin. This was an impossible goal in 1821, but one which foreshadowed the future. Its impracticality stemmed at least in part from the character of the regimes in London and Paris, as much as from the daring scope of the hopes of the Mediterranean rebels. Liberals and radicals in Spain, Naples and Turin – so divided over internal matters – were united in the vain hope that Spain would put itself at the head of a 'Mediterranean revolution' in 1821.

It must be remembered that these events were not the only aspects determining international relations in these decades. Rivalries of a more traditional kind divided Austria from Russia in the Balkans. The Balkans could even make allies of Britain and Russia, the most ideologically diverse powers in Europe. Even in Spain, Britain and France fell out soon after the end of the first Carlist War in their different efforts to influence the marriage of the young Spanish Queen, Isabel II. Support for liberal Spain never stopped the British from purloining as much as possible of the crumbling Spanish empire for her commercial expansion.

However, set beside this must be the continued efforts of Metternich to minimise rivalries in the Balkans in his efforts to keep the Holy Alliance – and the whole Congress System – together. Later, by the 1830s, the new liberal regimes of Britain and

France discerned a common enemy in Carlism in much the same way as Metternich viewed Jacobinism. The shadow of the French Revolution was very long, for all sides. By 1848–49, the signs were that the world of diplomacy was no longer coloured by these considerations. Manin and Cattaneo waited in vain for French intervention in these months, as did the Poles; Prussia and Austria acted together to restore order in central Europe, but did nothing to oppose the election of a Bonaparte to the presidency of a republican France, or, indeed, the proclamation of a new republic in Paris, the very heartland of subversion. By 1848, it seemed that the unthinkable had at last become tolerable. No one came forward to save Louis-Philippe. Such inaction, whether from Left or Right, would have been impossible earlier in the period. Internally, this failure to act dissolved an important source of unity between the disparate elements of Left and Right, as witnessed in Paris in April – May, 1848, when the radical political clubs committed to aiding the Poles were ignored not only by liberals in the government, but by the socialists as well. International revolution or counter-revolution had little meaning for either Left or Right as a whole by the time of 1848. It was no longer a source of unity either across borders or within the political divisions inside them.

(ii) Working for victory: hopes, fears and preludes to revolution
In general, the fear of revolution bound conservatives and reactionaries to each other, while its prospect could bring together liberals and radicals, but usually only if this prospect sprang from opposition to the likelihood of a true, reactionary counter-revolution which would threaten them both. Broadly, these were the conditions that fused conservatism and reaction into the Right, and liberalism and radicalism into the Left. Only in times of stress do these wider terms gain any real relevance.

On what might be termed the Right, the cause of unity usually originated with the conservatives. In most cases, they were the men most closely linked to power and also those least certain of their grip on it. Reactionaries were usually more confident of the loyalty of the popular classes to the existing order, or at least surer that it could be retrieved if recourse was made to their ideas. Thus, it was their self-assigned task to keep the reactionaries on their side, not merely to restrain their excesses. Conservatives had powerful cards in their hands in this process, especially their shared loyalty to ruling dynasties and to the general concepts of monarchy and aristocracy.

The epitomes of conservative success in achieving and then maintaining this general sense of unity on the Right are the examples of Prussia after 1818, when the departure of von Hardenberg opened the way for a reconciliation between the conservative bureaucracy and the *Jünkers* in the provincial estates, and the long Tory administration of Lord Liverpool and his successors, between 1812 and 1827. In both these cases, the coalition survived many difficult moments partly because conservatives curbed their own reforming instincts, but even more through shared loyalties to the ruling dynasty, a national Church and a common cultural and social experience. The elections of November 1820 in France were interpreted as the emergence of a similar secure base of the Right, prematurely as it transpired. However, the initial response of the propertied electorate to the assassination of the Duc de Berry and the mounting crisis in Spain, was to rally around the dynasty by returning a lower chamber dominated by conservatives and a large body of reactionaries who showed themselves ready to work with conservative ministers, Richelieu and Villèle, successively.

Metternich worked very hard to promote a comparable kind of unity, coupled with compromise and restraint, in the rather different political circumstances of the Italian states, where he supported the efforts of Consalvi in the Papal State, and of Dei Medici in the Kingdom of the Two Sicilies, to steer a course away from extremism while dissuading the reactionaries from open opposition to conservative ministers. In general, he was unsuccessful in this, as is revealed by his failure to prevent the election of the reactionary Pope Leo XII in 1823, which led to the dismissal of Consalvi, and by his inability to help Dei Medici master his avowed rival, Prince Canosa. In these two cases, conservative statesmen were undone not by radical revolution or the much vaunted conspiracies of the sects, but by their rivals on the Right. In these cases, reactionaries remained undaunted by the prospect that disunity could usher in the Left.

The early stages of the first Carlist War in Spain offer another interesting example of a conservative leader, Don Carlos, striving to create a broad front of the Right in the face of a liberal revolution. Ultimately, it proved impossible to hold together a coalition of conservatives wedded to the concept of a centralised state and reactionaries in quest of their lost regional autonomy. The breach probably culminated in the defection of the conservative General Maroto to the liberals at the Treaty of Vergara in 1839. However, the initial appeal to the Church and the legitimate king against a constitution imposed by a palace coup proved successful, and the Carlist coalition assembled itself with remarkable spontaneity.

When the unity of the Right cracked, disaster often loomed and the predictions of conservative observers were often proved correct, less through a vast swell of popular support for the Left, than through its higher degree of unity. This was the case in both Britain and France in the crises of *c.* 1826–30 and, in more extreme and very different circumstances, during the first Carlist War in Spain. The refusal of many reactionary members of Parliament to support Wellington and Peel over Catholic Emancipation in 1827 opened the way for the collapse of the long period of conservative rule, culminating in the passing of the First Reform Act in 1832. Similarly, the first major breaches in the ministry of Villèle came not from the Left, but from the defection of Chateaubriand and a large body of Ultra deputies, leaving the ministry exposed to attacks from the liberals, a process which ended in the revolution of July, 1830.

All these examples reveal the fragility and transience of unity between reactionaries and conservatives and, thus, the limited usefulness of the blanket term, 'Right', in the politics of the period. Yet, these cases also illuminate its importance at times of crisis and the very solid basis it could provide for a conservative regime, when it could be achieved for any length of time. Above all, the concept of a 'Right' as opposed to a 'Left' was very much alive in the minds of many conservative statesmen and to a lesser extent – often a crucially lesser one – in those of reactionaries.

The prospect of revolution could unite liberals and radicals to an unprecedented degree. Indeed, it is probably in the periods leading up to outbreaks of revolutionary activity and in the first phases of the crises, that the distinctions between them are most blurred. Perhaps the clearest example of this came in France, in the years between the election of 1827, which brought down the conservative government of Villèle, and the revolution of July, 1830. France had a representative, elective political system, a fact which makes it easier to trace the course of opposition because it took place in an open forum. The period 1827–30 was one of intense political activity, punctuated by a series of ferociously contested elections between the supporters of Charles X and the liberal opposition. Only avowed monarchists and advocates of the Charter were allowed by law to contest elections, thus radicals and republicans were excluded from formal politics. However, these elections provide a good example of radicals and liberals consciously sinking their differences against the perceived threat from Charles X. Many radical journals and other organisations took an active part in organising support for liberal candidates, even though they would derive no direct benefit from their efforts. A not dissimilar set of circumstances occurred in Britain, in the course of the campaign to pass the First Reform Act, between 1830 and 1832. Again, many radical elements on the fringes of parliamentary politics, composed of men who were not guaranteed access to any extension of the franchise, agitated vigorously on behalf of the Whig-Liberal ministry of Grey and Russell.

The leaders of the secret societies that flourished in Italy during the first years of the Restoration, notably those inspired by Buonarotti, guarded their plans carefully not only from Metternich's secret police, but from their own members. There was a practical reason for this, specifically to keep liberal and radical elements united. The sects probably contained as many liberals as radicals – driven to secrecy through fear of reaction more than a taste for revolution – and it was essential that they were kept unaware of the democratic ideology of the central leadership. This reveals not just the bizarre nature of the sects themselves, but also the sensitivity of their leaders to the clear ideological differences within the Left, and their potential for divisiveness.

By 1848, liberals and radicals were able to join forces and on the whole, to maintain their unity on an unprecedented scale. There were few traces of division along traditional lines in Paris, first in the crisis of February, when the liberals laid aside their attachment to an electorate based on a limited franchise to permit the adoption of a constitution that enshrined the classic radical demand for universal manhood suffrage. The ease with which this took place has often been overlooked in the light of later divisions. Yet even in the turmoil of the June Days, when faced by a true artisan revolt, driven by demands closer to early socialism than those of the Jacobin tradition, most radicals stood by their liberal allies and

113

opposed the rising. It was only in the last phases of the Second Republic that they turned on each other, when faced by the prospect of Louis-Napoleon's new form of authoritarianism.

In northern Italy, too, the early stages of 1848–49 saw considerable unity between liberals and radicals. In Venice and Milan, they served together in the provisional governments set up to oppose Austrian rule; as if to emphasise the point, the government of Milan was headed by the leading liberal theorist, Carlo Cattaneo, and that of Venice by the arch-radical, Daniel Manin. Here, too, unity was preserved to a remarkable degree in the face of the common enemy, Austria, and the difference with many earlier attempts at revolution is notable for this. The early stages of the 1848 revolutions in Germany also reveal a marked capacity for liberals and radicals to work together. The 'preparliament' which convoked the Frankfurt parliament, like the February provisional government in Paris, also embraced the cardinal demand of the radicals for the introduction of universal manhood suffrage. Even though this was, in effect, ignored during the elections to the Frankfurt parliament and in many corresponding elections to the diets of the constitutional states, radicals and liberals often continued to work together until the work of the parliament began.

These many examples bear out the capacity for a common enemy, usually the threat of counter-revolution and increasingly that of pre-Marxian socialism, to forge bonds between habitual rivals. It would be wrong to assume that liberal-radical alliances were always of a purely negative kind, however. Although nationalism was not responsible for the good relations between Milan and Venice, or the internal unity of these two governments, the case of Hungary certainly shows the ability of nationalism to bring various elements of the Left together in a crisis. The real binding force was probably more subtle, at least in the two great liberal states, Britain and France, and probably in Spain as well. On the one hand, this was the ability of the radicals to adapt to the role of a loyal parliamentary opposition when given the chance, as they were in Britain and Spain in the 1830s, and in France, fleetingly, in 1848–49 – although the radicals had been encouraged to believe they would be welcomed into the political fold by many liberals during the July Monarchy.

Conclusion

Revolution: the pressures of power

Inevitably, the many revolutions of the period were the work of those outside power which usually meant the liberals, sometimes the reactionaries and always and inevitably, radicals, nationalists, and socialists. When successful, these risings brought those on the fringes of politics to the centre of power, however briefly. Often, success in the early stages of the revolution transformed the alliances and ideological assumptions that had underlain them in the shadows of opposition, frequently to the detriment of the rebels.

In his seminal book written in 1953, *The Anatomy of Revolution*, Crane Brinton set out a powerful theory he termed 'the natural history of revolution'. Brinton's theory is predicated on the existence of a clear distinction between liberals (or moderates) and radicals (or extremists) which becomes more fundamental as the revolution develops. The natural course of a revolution moves from an initial phase dominated by liberals to a period of crisis, when the radicals seize power and drive the revolution further to the left until they, in turn, are overthrown by a renewed liberal faction who have moved further to the right. Brinton's theory was based on his analysis of the French Revolution of 1789, and is difficult to apply as a whole to those of 1820–23, 1830 or 1848–50, partly because they were so much shorter than that of 1789–99, but even more because their internal histories do not always follow Brinton's chronology. As has been seen, the revolutions which followed the great Revolution of 1789 were not hermetically sealed behind their respective national borders. Rather, they interacted with each other and were influenced by events elsewhere to a remarkable degree. It is also arguable that in many cases, radicals and nationalists began the risings and were more prominent in the whole process than Brinton's model allows. The whole process was often compressed. Radical and liberal elements vied for power simultaneously, and liberals might have to wrest power from radicals from the outset, never really gaining full control. Nor did the revolutions last long enough for liberals to regain power from radicals; there was no 'third phase'. Instead, foreign intervention or, in the case of France in 1849–50, indigenous counter-revolution cut short the process.

Nevertheless, Brinton's basic premise – of a growing, ultimately unbridgeable gulf between liberals and radicals, and simply of the

115

existence of two groups so defined within the revolution – does much to illuminate the revolutions of the Restoration period. It does even more to explain the ideological differences between them, in action.

The revolutions of 1821 are particularly important examples of the prominent place radicals occupied from the outset. They were initiated by small, well organised groups of army officers, most of whom were members of the more radical secret societies, the *Carbonari* in Naples and the *Comuneros* in Spain. This meant that the radicals actually controlled the first phase of these revolutions; in this way, they were able to impose the Spanish Constitution of 1812 on their respective states, before the liberals could formulate alternatives. However, what followed was a gradual usurpation of the revolution by the liberals, partly because they did better than the radicals in the elections, partly because the radicals had less experience of government than their more moderate allies. In Naples, the two factions drew back together only in the face of Austrian intervention, in the last days of the struggle, while in Spain, the radicals tightened their grip on power and became ever more extreme in the face of growing opposition. In both cases, and in that of Piedmont where the divisions became even clearer, the experience of these revolutions exposed the deep rifts between liberals and radicals that the secrecy of the sects had sought to conceal. It also discredited the model of the Spanish Constitution of 1812 in the eyes of the liberals. They had accepted it with reservations, partly from expediency, but also because they hoped that its system of indirect representation would balance with its insistence on universal manhood suffrage. Henceforth, it was regarded as a vehicle for radical politics by most liberals.

The revolutions of 1830 are among the most elusive political events of the period and, as Clive Church has pointed out in his study of them, Brinton's model of 'natural revolution' has even less application to their courses than to those of 1820. However, although they were too short to encompass distinctly liberal and radical phases, their outcomes were deeply influenced by the ideological categories of the period. As has been seen, at least in states with representative governments, the revolutions followed hard upon periods when fear of reaction galvanised liberals and radicals into broad coalitions to protect themselves. When the defining crisis came, as Church observes, it was largely induced by the governments themselves, who forced the pace of events to-wards confrontation. Thus, although the revolutions occurred with the aid of those outside conventional politics, they were not initiated by them, in sharp contrast to those of 1820. Thus, the lib-eral opposition never lost control of the process, being close enough to the centre of power already to be able to seize it and shape new regimes according to its own ideas.

In specifically political terms – judged by the regimes they pro-duced – the revolutions of 1830 in France and Belgium, together with the crisis in Britain and the subsequent creation of a constitu-tional monarchy in Spain, mark the high tide of liberalism in west-ern Europe. Their very success, in these terms, ensured that a split with the radicals was inevitable but along with it, came the eclipse of reaction as a powerful force in contemporary politics. In the widening range of constitutional states, the 1830s saw national politics transformed into a process of amalgamation of conserva-tives and liberals. Those regimes which survived 1848–49 un-scathed were those who also accommodated the radicals, as in Britain and Spain. Those who rejected them most fiercely – as in France and the southern German states – fared worst. Initially, in almost every case, the key to understanding the political compo-nent of the revolutions of 1830 is the awareness by all those con-cerned of the shades of ideology which separated allies and adver-saries, alike. In many cases, the broader coalitions of Left and Right scarcely survived the last gunshots, so clear had they be-come even before the crises erupted. Whatever their claims to a wider significance, the 1830 revolutions are instructive as lessons in ideological awareness.

The political alignments and the ideologies that underpinned the earlier revolutions of the Restoration period unravelled alto-gether in the final phases of the revolutions of 1848–49, when a 'party of order' emerged to create a new Right which embraced many liberals and even some radicals alongside conservatives and reactionaries. Simultaneously, the old Left fragmented or, more precisely, radicalism fragmented, as the rift with socialism was brought home in an urban context. Those radicals not absorbed into the 'party of order' – probably the majority – found it impossi-ble to work with liberals, turning their energies specifically to-wards nationalism in some cases, as with Manin, or to the pursuit of traditional radical goals in the countryside, as was so often the case in France. These revolutions, so often seen as ushering in new forces, saw in fact the dissolution of the political world which preceded them and its realignment. The most resilient of its elements – nationalism, Marxist socialism, economic liberalism, and reforming conservatism – would be transformed in the decades which followed this shattering of the political culture that evolved between the Congress of Vienna and 1848. Radicals, liberals, socialists and nationalists had, indeed, responded to the initial crises by standing together in most cases, but over most of Europe, when the broad coalitions of Left and Right disintegrated, they did so in new ways, scattering their component parts in directions different from any seen before.

The revolutions of 1848–51 did, indeed, change the face of European political life forever, but not in ways the revolutionaries intended or that conservatives or reactionaries had predicted. They shattered the existing political order in every country where serious disorder occurred. Instead of creating new radical regimes influenced by nationalism or socialism – as they were then generally understood – they gave birth to a new form of conservatism, able to absorb elements of liberalism, nationalism and even socialism, and to transform them almost beyond recognition.

The end of an era

It would be inaccurate, and probably misleading, to attribute too great a degree of continuity to the evolution of political ideologies in the early nineteenth century. Nevertheless, the behaviour of the leading groups of participants of the revolutions of the period in relation to each other denote a process of evolution in operation, however convoluted in more peaceful periods. It was a process that would bequeath the labels of the period to future generations, but not their original substance. In short, the revolutions were a series of signposts that led to a new political order where the politics of the early nineteenth century would become almost, if not quite, obsolete.

This is what makes the political thought of this period so deceptive to the eyes of later generations. A series of coherent political traditions emerged in the course of these decades, each with its attendant discourse, all of which referred to those of their rivals. However, these traditions and the discourses they spawned were drawn from the immediate past, from the French Revolution and the old order it challenged. They were backward looking, referential. As a result, they changed and developed in direct response to their own times, but always within the context of the recent past.

All the political ideologies of the period were based on the assumption that the state was intrinsically weak unless deliberately bolstered by reform. It was a question not only of whether this course was desirable, but whether it was even feasible. Few eras of political history have bequeathed a richer vocabulary – a richer discourse – to their successors, yet few generations of politicians have been so quickly outstripped by changes beyond the realm of politics, in this case by the gathering momentum of advances in technology, especially in transportation and warfare.

It must be remembered that the social and cultural results of these material changes, often – if now less frequently – labelled the Industrial Revolution, only caught up with them by the last decade or so of the period. Much more obvious to contemporaries were the major changes in transportation and military technology, especially in northern and western Europe. By the 1830s, these were in clear evidence; railways, steamships and better roads together with more powerful rifles, better artillery and the telegraph combined to make the state more powerful than had been dreamed of at time of the Congress of Vienna.

That previous assumptions about the State were beginning to change is evident in the suppression of socialist agitation in France after the revolution of 1830 and also, perhaps, in the more gradual stifling of the Carlist revolt in Spain, in the course of the 1830s. By the revolutions of 1848–51, it was brutally obvious that these very specific technological changes – quite different from the more uneven, diffuse changes to the economy – had reversed assumptions about the state in particular, and politics in general. It is increasingly clear that in the second phase of these revolutions in 1849, the radicals gained a significant degree of support not only in large capital cities such as Paris, Berlin or Vienna, but in many parts of the countryside as well. Despite both the scale of this support and the fact that it was often found in hitherto isolated rural areas, the new technology ensured that these revolts were suppressed quickly as well as ruthlessly. The state was there to be used and abused by whoever could seize the levers of power; the question of curbing its powers was now an ethical point, a deliberate choice. This had not really been the central issue before mid-century and, logically, the essence of politics in the early nineteenth century does not reflect it.

The years 1814–51 form a most singular historical period. The Restoration was poised between the French Revolution and the material changes of mid-century, enveloped by unprecedented international calm, it appears now as an era as unique and self contained in its contours as might be found in the general mess of human affairs. It is ironic that it bequeathed the outward trappings of its political culture, and so little of the context in which they were conceived.

Selected documents

Document 1

The Congress of Vienna set about redrawing the map of Europe in 1814–15 and has often been criticised for the lack of attention it paid to nationalist aspirations, particularly in the German and Italian states. However, the real source of the protests that reached the Congress often had nothing to do with nationalism, as such. Rather, they came from those states which had their hopes of regaining independence dashed in the reorganisation. This protest came from the leaders of the ancient Italian city-state of Genoa, which Napoleon annexed to France in 1805. The Congress then gave it to the King of Piedmont-Savoy in 1814. It is found in the State Archives of Turin.

Genoa, 26 December, 1814. The President of the Government of Genoa.

> We accepted the reins of government in the hopes of restoring our dear fatherland to its original splendour ... in the hope that the rights of a people to their independence, which dates from the beginnings of their history, might be set before the right of conquest ... It is time that the Great Powers respect their independence, and that a solemn treaty re-establish the old equilibrium of Europe ... It only remains for us to fulfil the sad and honourable duty to protest that the right of Genoa to independence might remain unrecognised, but they cannot be extinguished.

Document 2

This is taken from *Mémoires d'Outre Tombe*, volume III, book vi, the autobiography of the French reactionary politician, Chateaubriand, describing his reasons for breaking with the conservative government of Villèle, in 1824, and his adoption of direct opposition to it. Rather than dwelling on the specific political reasons for this, Chateaubriand puts forward a clear example of the influence of British ideas on the parliamentary life of Restoration France.

> My concept of representative government led me into opposition; systematic opposition seems to me the only kind (of opposition) fitting to this government; opposition according to *conscience* is impotent ... (it) consists of floating between parties ... of voting according to circumstances ... In so far as England has been stable, it has been when it has had only a systematic opposition: one enters and leaves (office) together with one's friends; on leaving government, one sits on the opposition benches ... If men are only the representatives of principles, systematic opposition will only produce its principles when it sets itself to opposing *men*.

Document 3

Luigi Minichini was a Neapolitan *Carbonaro* and a former priest who took an active part in the revolution of 1820 against the Bourbons and then fled to Spain when the revolution collapsed. He fought with the Spanish constitutional forces until their defeat by the forces of the Congress powers and then fled to exile in Britain. He wrote his reflections on the revolutions of 1820 in Birmingham, in 1838, *Chronicle of a Revolution*. These are his thoughts on the need for open, accountable government and freedom of expression, which represent the views of many contemporary liberals and radicals.

> Convinced by reason ... and experience, I believe firmly that an absolute monarch might be able to make a nation happy, where his wisdom and justice make him just and accessible ... Even supposing his existence, could he hold all the reins of government? The ministers would be responsible only to the monarch (to say nothing of how they might be chosen). The abuse of their powers is virtually inevitable ... This alone ... makes their administration accountable only to the king; this is more than enough to convince anyone that

the government of an absolute prince ... is of necessity oppressive of the rights of the nation and ruins its happiness ... Hereditary, absolute monarchy is a real evil.

Document 4

Following several disturbances by students and radical secret societies in 1819, notably the 'Warburg Festival', ten states of the German Confederation met at Karlsbad. There, Metternich urged upon them stricter controls on freedom of expression, directed against radical and nationalist elements, which were, in fact, restricted to a few intellectuals. The Karlsbad Decrees of September, 1820, represent the severe nature of conservative repression in the early years of the Restoration, just as the focus of those decrees reveals the narrow basis of support such 'subversives' actually had. This extract is from the 'University Law', which together with the 'Press Law' and the creation of a police and censorship commission for the German states, were the core of the decrees. It is reprinted in *Documents in the Political History of the European Continent, 1815–1939*, Oxford, 1968, pp. 67–8.

The University Law
1   The Sovereign (prince of each state) shall make choice for each university of an extraordinary commissioner, furnished with suitable instructions and powers, residing in the place where the university is established ...

The duty of the commissioner shall be to watch over the most rigorous observation of the laws and disciplinary regulations; to observe carefully the spirit with which the professors are guided ... and to devote constant attention to everything which may tend to the maintenance of morality, good order and decency among the youths ...

2   The Governments of the States (of the German Confederation) reciprocally engage to remove from their universities ... the professors ... against whom it may be proved that in ... abusing their legitimate influence over the minds of youth, by the propagation of pernicious dogmas, hostile to order and tranquillity, or in sapping the foundations of existing institutions ... A professor thus excluded may not be admitted in any other State of the (German) Confederation to any other establishment of public instruction.

3   The laws long since made against secret or unauthorised associations at the universities shall be maintained in all their force and

rigour, and shall be particularly extended with so much the more severity against the well-known society formed some years ago ... the *Burscehnschaft* ...

Document 5

Alexis de Tocqueville was one of the few liberal thinkers of the early nineteenth century to fear the growing power of the central-ised state, and to have doubts about the extension of democracy to the creation of representative, parliamentary institutions. These doubts were confirmed by the course of the 1848 revolution in France. This extract is from his famous book, *The Ancien Regime and the French Revolution*, written in the aftermath of 1848. It re-veals the pessimism of many liberals, after 1848, and the passing of their political world. The translation is from Stuart Gilbert's edi-tion, of 1969.

There may be some to accuse me of making overmuch of liberty – that watchword of the past. Nowadays, so I am told, no one in France sets any store on it. All I would say ... in my defence is that my devotion to freedom is of very long standing ... Though there can be no certainty about the future three facts are plain to see in the light of past experience. First, that all our contemporaries are driven on by a force that we may hope to regulate or curb, but cannot over-come, and it is a force impelling them ... to the destruction of aristoc-racy. Secondly, that those peoples who are so constituted as to have the utmost difficulty in getting rid of despotic government ... are the ones in which aristocracy has ceased to exist and can no longer exist. Thirdly, that nowhere is despotism calculated to produce such evil effects as in social groups of this order (the popular classes); since, more than any other kind of regime, it fosters the growth of all the vices to which they are congenitally prone and, indeed, incites them to go farther still on the way to which their natural bent inclines them.

Document 6

In 1823, the German scholar and cultural nationalist, Jacob Grimm, reviewed a book of Serbian folk songs, collected by Vuk Karadžić, who is regarded as the intellectual founder of Serbian national consciousness. Vuk was an active politician and a rebel leader, but his great work was the preservation of Serb cultural traditions. This extract is taken from Appendix D of Duncan Wilson's *The Life and Times of Vuk Stefanovi Karadžić, (1787–1864),* Ann Arbor, 1986. It reveals both the peasant, traditionalist character of Serb nationalism, and the deep interest taken in this approach to nationalism by Grimm, thus offering a point of contact between western, intellectual nationalism and peasant culture.

These Serbian popular songs are not the result of laborious research in old manuscripts, but have all been recorded from the living voice of the people; perhaps they have never been written down before, and in this sense they are not old, but they are likely to have a long life. Some of them ... celebrate deeds which happened not so much as twenty years ago; and one cannot detect that those concerned with the older and less definitely historical events of popular songs are any different in style and manner ... German folk-songs show the crudity of form usual in popular dialects; in their content there are artificialities and gaps which can easily be explained when we consider how long it is since the subjects represented have been eliminated from the environment of educated people. The Serbian popular songs on the other hand are couched in pure and noble language ... In the Serbian territories there are no crude vulgarities of popular expression, at least not in the blatant forms common here in Germany. [Grimm's own note: Degenerate and mixed forms occur perhaps only in towns, where Turks, Germans and other foreigners live or the clergy try to impose their obsolescent church language; in the country everyone speaks purely.] ... We should not be surprised by the absence of the coarse and common elements in the Serbian language; a thousand years ago and less, things were the same in Germany. Just as now in Serbia there is no divergence between the poor peasant and the respectable man in purity of language, and just as the men of Herzegovina keep their native way of speech, so with us formerly ... Probably as soon as Serbia attains culture ... the age of those epic songs will be over ...

Document 7

Marx wrote *The Class Struggle in France* in the immediate aftermath of the revolution of 1848–50. Many of its assertions were wrong, and Marx was quick to correct the most blatant. However, his assessment of the July Monarchy of 1830–48, given here, reflected the views of many radicals – and, indeed, many reactionaries – as well as socialists. It presents a negative view of a regime generally acknowledged by contemporaries to be a classic example of a liberal government.

It was not the French bourgeoisie that ruled under Louis Philippe, but one faction of it: bankers, stock-exchange kings, owners of coal and iron mines and forests, a part of the landed proprietors associated with them – the so-called finance aristocracy. It sat on the throne, it dictated laws in the Chambers, it distributed public offices ... The industrial bourgeoisie proper formed part of the official opposition, that is, it was represented only as a minority in the Chambers...

The July monarchy was nothing but a joint-stock company for the exploitation of France's national wealth, the dividends of which were divided among ministers, Chambers (the parliament), 240,000 voters and their adherents. Louis-Philippe was the director of this company ... Trade, industry, agriculture, shipping, the interests of the industrial bourgeoisie, were bound to be continually endangered and prejudiced under this system. Cheap government ... was what it had inscribed in the July Days (of 1830) on its banner.

Since the finance aristocracy made the laws, was at the head of the administration of the state, had command of all the organised public authorities, dominated public opinion ... the same prostitution, the same shameless cheating, the same mania to get rich was repeated in every sphere ... to get rich not by production, but by pocketing the already available wealth of others. Clashing every moment with the bourgeois laws themselves, an unbridled assertion of unhealthy and dissolute appetites manifested itself, particularly at the top of bourgeois society.

Document 8

Mazzini wrote *Interests and Principles* in the winter of 1835–36, during his first exile in Switzerland. In this extract, he sets out the core of his concept of what it means to belong to a nation, a people. He also sets out what sets his ideas apart from liberals, radicals and socialists, while also drawing attention to those beliefs they had in common. Mazzini stresses the importance of beliefs held in common, in his search for the 'social cement' of nationalism. Although written comparatively early in his career, *Interests and Principles* embodies his central ideas. The translation is from G. Mazzini, *The Duties of Man and Other Essays*, T. Jones, ed., London, 1955 edn.

Instil into a People's soul, or into its teachers and writers, one single principle, and it will be worth more to that People and Country than a whole system of interests and rights addressed to each individual; or a war to the death against the acts of a corrupt government.

If by dint of example you can root in a nation's heart the principle which the French Revolution proclaimed but never carried out, that *the State owes every member the means of existence or the chance to work for it*, and add a fair definition of existence, you have prepared the triumph of right over privilege; the end of the monopoly of one class over another, and the end of pauperism; for which at present there are only palliatives, Christian charity, or cold and brutal maxims like those of the English school of political economists (the radical Utilitarians).

When you have raised men's minds to believe in the other principle: *that society is an association of labours* ... you will have no more castes, no more aristocracies, or civil wars, or crises. You will have a *People*.

And when the Gospel of brotherhood of all the men of a nation has made the soul a sanctuary of virtue and love; when the great conception of Nationality is no more dwarfed to mean proportions; than mere material interest, interest that always has its rivals ... and when woman ... teaches her offspring heavenly truths ... then only will you have a nation such as you can never have from sophists who would found a Godless Nationality. For Nationality is belief in a common origin and end ...

Document 9

John Stuart Mill was arguably the most important theorist of English radicalism. In the course of the 1840s, he moved away from the Utilitarianism of Jeremy Bentham and, not unlike Tocqueville, began to develop a suspicion of the power of the state. He wrote *On Liberty* in 1859, and it might serve as a reflection on the central political debates of the early nineteenth century. His renewed concern for the rights of the individual might be seen as a return to the earlier, liberal roots of radicalism. This extract is from J. S. Mill, *Utilitarianism*, M. Warnock, ed., Glasgow, 1962 edn.

Society can and does execute its own mandates: and if it issues wrong mandates instead of right, or any mandates at all in things with which it ought not to meddle, it practises a social tyranny more formidable than many kinds of political oppression, since ... it leaves fewer means of escape, penetrating much more deeply into the details of life, and enslaving the soul itself. Protection, therefore, against the tyranny of the magistrate is not enough: there needs protection also against the tyranny of the prevailing opinion and feeling; against the tendency of society to impose, by other means than civil penalties, its own ideas and practices as rules of conduct on those who dissent from them; to fetter the development, and if possible, prevent the formation, of any individuality not in harmony with its ways, and compels all characters to fashion themselves upon the model of its own. There is a limit to the legitimate interference of collective opinion with individual independence: and to find that limit, and maintain it against encroachment, is as indispensable to a good condition of human affairs, as protection against political despotism.

Document 10

The future king of the French, Louis-Philippe, paid close attention to the restoration of his cousin, Louis XVIII, in 1814. When still Duke of Orléans, he analysed the Charter of 1814, and the king's attitude towards it, in some detail. This extract is taken from his *Memoires of 1814*, in the Archives Nationales de Paris, (Papiers de la Maison de France, 300-Archives Privées-III-13).

... Louis XVIII recognised ... and it was impossible for him to fail to do so, that everything that had been accomplished in France since 1789, whether the most important legislative acts or the pettiest administrative decisions, were maintained in full force, without exception. Yet, what proved damaging to him, and to France, was that he did not perceive that the purpose of all the new laws was, invariably, to weaken royal authority, and to diminish all the privileges and attributes of royalty; thus, to obliterate completely the old organisation of the kingdom, and put in place of our monarchical institutions, disfigured copies or false imitations of those of England and the United States. It did not take great foresight to see that the Revolutionary storm ... had left only imperfect, inexact and often bitter memories ... which created fear at the sight of the restoration of old institutions. Yet, at the same time, France, exhausted by everything it had endured ... called in one voice for the establishment of a constitutional monarchy, which was not to be the old order, but a new monarchy adapted to the spirit of the age, to the advance of civilisation ...

Document 11

During the First Carlist War of the 1830s, in Spain, it was common for local Carlist commanders to issue proclamations to stir up support for the rebellion. In 1837, in the province of Catalonia, the Carlist leader Vicente Pou issued a manifesto remarkable for its ideological coherence. It embodies many of the major preoccupations of Carlism. It is taken from A. Bullón de Mendoza, *La Primera Guerra Carlista*, Madrid, 1992, pp. 560–2. Proclamations of this kind often offer the best evidence of the ideology of popular reactionary movements.

... Policies which alter the laws of the state without need or utility are found most often when they are influenced by other nations; there is general agreement to reject these changes, as they shock public opinion; Holy Religion is the ultimate, sublime principle of the people, who desire a pious prince, who will restore the old ways and revive the blessed days of our fathers ... Don Carlos, protected by God, will defeat the revolution, and under his paternal rule, we will see the hoped for restoration; the restoration of principles and doctrines, of laws and institutions, of habits, of customs ... The Holy Faith in all its dignity and purity; the sovereignty of the king, without the checks that destroy it or hinder his good deeds; ... the vigour of the old laws and *fueros* (local and provincial privileges); the extinction of administrative abuses and vices; the noble and honourable independence of the Nation and the prosperity of all classes: these are his aims ... We turn to religion as the basic foundation of society and we see the legitimate authority of the prince as its powerful and healthy influence on society, the best and most secure guarantee against the fury of popular passions and the degradation of true liberty ... by tyranny ... What is irrational or extremist in this? ... that the monarchy might be made strong through a united sovereign will of the people rather than by armed force and a mass of civil servants; that the abuses of public administration which enrage the people and the excesses that warp and corrupt the government be destroyed. There is no surer road to these ends than the preservation of old, essentially conservative institutions ... (We demand) nothing more than to be left in active possession of our immemorial legitimate rights; and that, in accord with the wise counsel of public law, no innovations be introduced without grave need ...

Document 12

Liberalism reached its apogee in Spain by the 1840s, when the Moderate Party dominated political life. Early in 1848, a moderate deputy in Parliament, Juan Bravo Murillo, stated his support for the kind of narrow electorate which characterised the liberal regimes of the 1830, 1840s and 1850s, in most of western Europe. This extract is taken from the minutes of the parliamentary session of 30 January, 1848 – only a few days before the collapse of the July Monarchy in France and the start of the 1848 revolutions – and is reproduced in *Historia de España*, R. Menendez Pidal, ed., vol. 34, *La Era Isabellina y el Sexenio Democrático (1834–74)*, Madrid, 1981, p. 392.

> It is my opinion that the electors must be few in number ... Among the (present) electors are many who only just attain the qualities and character necessary in an elector, and there are others who are much wealthier. Who are those who want the vote, in reality? The lowest of the low; those who pay very little (in taxes). Vote? Them? No, gentlemen; the rich must vote, the influential (must vote). Let us suppose that universal (manhood) suffrage is established. Who will vote then? The wealthiest and most influential of all, those with the most power; because each influential person in a town or a region has his 'clients', his hirelings, his workmen, people he employs and others who look to him for favours and protection; the influential, the rich, the landowner, one or more in every town, is the one who will control the most (votes); and when they put his voting papers in the urne, people will vote as the most influential man tells them to. This is the truth: everybody knows it, everybody knows about it. I want to reach the truth by the shortest route.

Document 13

The Frankfurt Assembly was flooded with petitions from the German artisans and their associations, demanding a halt to the wholesale introduction of liberal economic ideas, particularly freedom of profession and free trade. The petition of the trades-

men of Karlsruhe is very direct in its attack on *laissez-faire* economics. It is reproduced in by P. H. Noyes in *Organisation and Revolution. Working-Class Associations in the German Revolutions of 1848–
1849*, Princeton, 1966, p. 240.

> Only theoreticians who do not know the internal conditions of in-
> dustry and its needs, only people who find nourishment in unlim-
> ited freedom for their own flightiness without thinking of the fu-
> ture, only speculators and the aristocrats of money who snatch some
> advantage for themselves out of the frivolity and need of others,
> speak with scorn of a legal order in industry and praise unlimited
> freedom of trade as a means to higher development, as a source of
> well being; while the professional with insight, supported by expe-
> rience and instructed by facts, finds and sees in the unlimited free-
> dom of trade the decline of the middling class, the disproportionate
> increase of the proletariate and the almost exorbitant burden of sup-
> porting the poor in the community which arise from this.

Document 14

Camillo Benso di Cavour would become the second constitutional
prime minister of Piedmont-Sardinia, after the revolution of 1848–
49, and the first prime minister of a united Italy, in 1860. He spent
most of the 1830s and 1840s in discreet opposition to the absolutist
monarchy of Charles-Albert IV, but watched the emerging
strength of liberal regimes, elsewhere. In August, 1834, he con-
fided to his private diary, his thoughts on the decision by the July
Monarchy in France to expand the legislation promoting free
trade. It is taken from C. Cavour, *Diari (1836–56)*, vol. I, ed. A.
Bogge, Rome, 1991, p. 166.

> It is with great satisfaction that I have seen him (the liberal deputy,
> Janvier) proclaim his determination to request freedom of com-
> merce. And yet the Carlists (the Ultras) take him for their spokes-
> men. They take for one of their guides (in economic affairs) one of
> the most enthusiastic apologists for the revolution of (17)89 ... In
> truth, this party (the Ultras) has gone mad ... The whole human race
> would have to be insane if it allowed them to impose ... their bizarre
> spectacle, which (supposes that) absolutism and demagogy are
> equally excellent things and that no good can come of a (political)
> system that tries to tempor them both, thus to assure the rule of en-
> lightenment and reason. Although there may be hardened Carlists,

there is no doubt that the vast majority of young men in the party will adopt the seductive doctrines of advanced liberalism, with enthusiasm and good faith ... (and) that they will, in years to come, extend and develop all those freedoms compatible with society as it actually is. Let us hope for this happy future. This hope is the only compensation for the intense distaste inspired by the absurd, shameful farces of the present (in Piedmont).

Bibliographical essay

For a subject covering almost four decades and an entire continent, it would be too ambitious to attempt a complete bibliography. In the main, this essay concentrates on works in English, save where the standard studies remain untranslated.

Before entering into the specific history of the nature of politics between 1814 and 1851, guidance on the general outline of the period can be found in the early chapters of R. Gildea, *Barricades and Borders. Europe, 1800-1914*, Oxford, 1987. Older, but still useful, I. Collins, *The Age of Progress, Europe, 1789-1870*, London, 1972 edn. Dated by its Marxism, but eternally stimulating is E. Hobsbawm, *The Age of Revolution*, London, 1971. There is a paucity of general books on the period 1814-51, itself; the best known being J. Droz, *Europe between Revolutions, 1815-48*, Glasgow, 1976 edn, now a far from adequate survey.

The diplomatic history of the period and the work of the Congress of Vienna are now served admirably by the magnificant P. W. Schroeder, *The Transformation of European Politics, 1763-1848*, Oxford, 1994, which supersedes all previous general studies. Still valuable are A. Sked, ed., *Europe's Balance of Power, 1815-48*, London, 1979; C. K. Webster, *The Congress of Vienna*, London, 1919. and H. Nicholson, *The Congress of Vienna*, London, 1948.

The national and regional histories of the period are well served. For France see: A. Jardin and A. Tudesq, *Restoration and Reaction, 1815-1848*, Eng. trans., Cambridge, 1983; G. Bertier de Savigny, *The Bourbon Restoration*, Eng. trans., Philadelphia, 1966; H. A. C. Collingham, *The July Monarchy, 1830-1848*, London, 1988. For a Marxist interpretation see: R. Magraw, *France, 1814-1915. The Bourgeois Century*, Oxford, 1983. A significant, sensitive study of the period, never translated into English or French, is A. Omodeo, *Studi sull'Età della Restaurazione*, Turin, 1974 edn, first published in several parts, between 1946 and 1948.

For the German states see: the relevant chapters of J. J. Sheehan, *German History, 1770-1866*, Oxford, 1989. T. S. Hamerow, *Restoration, Revolution, Reaction. Economics and Politics in Germany, 1815-71*, Princeton, 1958, is an older study, but contains useful information. On the Italian states: S. J. Woolf, *A History of Italy, 1700-1866*, London, 1979, is excellent. Also of interest is H. Hearder, *Italy in the Age of the Risorgimento*, London, 1983. On Spain see: R. Carr, *Spain, 1808-1939*, Oxford, 1991 edn. On the Habsburg lands: C. A. Macartney, *The Habsburg Empire, 1790-1918*, London, 1968, is irreplaceable. On the Balkans see: C. and B. Jelavich, *The Establishment of the Balkan National States, 1804-1920*, Berkley, 1977. Also, M. Petrovich, *A History of Modern Serbia*, Berkley, 1976, vol. I and N. Davies, *God's Playground. A History of Poland*, London, 1981, vol. I. On Britain see L. Colley, *Britons. Forging the Nation, 1707-1837*, New Haven, 1991, for a new, often inspired perspective and N. Gash, *Aristocracy and People, 1815-1865*, London, 1979, for a splendid standard account. Also see R. F. Foster, *Modern Ireland, 1600-1972*, London, 1988. On Russia, H. Seton-Watson, *The Russian Empire, 1801-1917*, Oxford, 1967, is the most detailed study. D. Saunders, *Russia in the Age of Reaction and Reform, 1801-1881*, London, 1992, is the best of the more recent studies, admirable for its emphasis on local history.

Literature on conservatism, as such, is comparatively rare, so bound up was it with practical politics. However, there are a number of very good modern studies which focus on aspects of its development. The final chapters of J. C. D. C. Clark, *English Society, 1688-1832*, Cambridge, 1985, are an excellent and welcome reassessment of English conservatism and reaction. N. Gash, *Lord Liverpool*, London, 1979, is an important contribution to the subject. R. D. Billinger, *Metternich and the German Question*, Newark, 1991, is a thoughtful study, as is the whole corpus of work by A. J. Reinerman on Austria and the Papal states; see especially, *Austria and the Papacy in the Age of Metternich*, 2 vols, Washington, 1979 and 1989. M. Raeff, *Michael Speransky: Statesman of Imperial Russia, 1772-1839*, The Hague, 1969 edn and J. Gooding, 'The liberalism of Michael Speransky', *Slavonic and East European Review*, 64, 1986, pp. 401-24, are important studies of the conflict between liberalism and conservatism, and should be read together, if possible. Also useful, in the context of Russia, is J. M. Hartley, *Alexander I*, London, 1994. For excellent studies of the interaction between liberalism, reaction and conservatism in the German states see: R. M. Berdahl, *The Politics of the Prussian Nobility. The development of a conservative ideology, 1770-1848*, Princton, 1988 and L. Lee, *The Politics of Harmony: Civil Service, Liberalism and Social Reform in Baden, 1800-1850*, Newark, 1980. M. Walker, *German Home Towns. Community, State and General Estate, 1648-1871*, Ithaca, 1971, is a classic study, emphaisising local history. J. Gillis, *The Prussian Bureaucracy in Crisis, 1840-1860*, Stanford, 1971 is perceptive on the interaction of liberalism and conservatism. On France, the work of Bertier de Sauvigny, cited above, approaches the period from a conservative point of view. R. Rémond, *The Right Wing in France from 1815 to De Gaulle*, Eng. trans. Philadelphia, 1969, places the conservatism of the Restoration in a wider perspective. One of the best general assessments of Metternich in English remains that by E. L. Woodward in *Three Studies in European Conservatism*, London, 1963 edn. Also valuable is E. Radvany, *Metternich's Projects for Reform in Austria*, The Hague, 1971, although not as comprehensive as its title suggests. D. E. Emerson, *Metternich and the Political Police*, New York, 1968, is an important study.

The classic, but highly partisan study of liberalism in the nineteenth century is G. De Ruggiero, *The History of European Liberalism*, Oxford, Eng. trans., 1966 edn. Few general studies have followed it, however. The work of Lenore O'Boyle takes a general perspective: 'The middle class in western Europe, 1815-1848', *American Historical Review*, 71, 1966, pp. 826-45 and 'The problem of an excess of educated men in Western Europe, 1800-1850', *Journal of Modern History*, 42, 1970 pp. 471-95. O'Boyle's views have been challenged by A. Cobban, in a purely French context, in 'The middle class in France, 1815-1848', *French Historical Studies*, 5, 1967, pp. 41-56; the same issue contains O'Boyle's reply. For the German states, the work of J. J. Sheehan is invaluable; see especially *German Liberalism in the Nineteenth Century*, Chicago, 1987, and 'Liberalism and Society in Germany, 1815-1848', *Journal of Modern History*, 45, 1973, pp. 583-604. A classic regional study remains J. Droz, *Le libéralism rhénan, 1815-1848*, Paris, 1940. On similar lines J. Diefendorf, *Businessmen and Politics in the Rhineland, 1789-1834*, Princeton, 1988. The work of L. Lee, cited above, is also useful in this context. For France, the standard biography of Guizot is by D. Johnson, *Guizot*, London, 1963. For Thiers: J. P. T. Bury and R. Tombs, *Thiers, 1797-1877, a political life*, London, 1986. The best life of Louis-Philippe in English remains T. E. B. Howarth, *Citizen-King*, London, 1957. Two recent studies in French are of great importance: G. Antonetti, *Louis-Philippe*, Paris, 1994, and above all, P. Ronsanvallon, *La Monarchie Impossible. Les Chartes de 1814 et de 1830*, Paris, 1994. An interesting approach to the politics of the early Restoration is A. Spitzer, *The French Generation of 1820*, Princeton, 1987. An excellent local study of Bologna, which concentrates on the growth of liberalism parallel to the failure of conservative reform in the Papal states is S. C. Hughes, *Crime, Disorder and the Risorgimento. The Politics of Policing in Bologna*, Cambridge, 1994, a more wide-ranging book than its title suggests. On the *Carbonari*, R. J. Rath, 'The Carbonary: their origins, initiation rites and aims', *American Historical Review*, 64, 1964. More wide-ranging and stimulating is J. M. Roberts, *The Mythology of the Secret Societies*, London, 1972. There are two good accounts in English of the Decembrist Movement in Russia: A. G. Mazour, *The First Russian Revolution, 1825*, Stanford, 1961 edn and M. Raeff, *The Decembrist Movement*, Englewood, 1966. These can be supplemented by W. B. Lincoln, 'A re-examination of some historical stereotypes: an analysis of the career patterns and backgrounds of the Decembrists', *Jahrbücher für Geschichte Osteuropas*, 24, 1976, pp. 357-68. On liberalism in Eastern Europe see, M. Kukiel, *Czartoryski and European Unity (1770-1861)*, Princeton, 1955, and W. H. Zawadzki, *A Man of Honour: Adam Czartoryski as a statesman of Russia and Poland, 1795-1831*, Oxford, 1993, a fine study. G. Barany, *Stephen Széchenyi and the Awakening of Hungarian Nationalism, 1791-1841*, Stanford, 1968. Among the huge literature on British liberalism, the classics remain M. Brock, *The Great Reform Act*, London, 1973, and D. C. Moore, *The Politics of Deference*, Oxford, 1976. N. Gash, *Mr. Secretary Peel*, London. 1961 and *Sir Robert Peel*, London, 1972, form an indispensable biography of the greatest liberal statesman of the period. See also his abridgement of them, *Peel*, London, 1977. There is an excellent literature on O'Connell; the recent is the masterly biography by O. Macdonagh, *O'Connell*, London, 1991. See also, A. Macintyre, *The Liberator: Daniel O'Connell and the Irish Party, 1830-1847*, London, 1965. G. Machin, *The Catholic Question in English Politics, 1820 to 1830*, Oxford, 1964, and F. O'Ferrall, *Catholic Emancipation: Daniel O'Connell and the birth of Irish democracy*, Dublin, 1985.

Reaction is seldom approached directly in studies of the period. One of its most important components was religion, both official and popular, and the following are invaluable in this respect: for an overview see, O. Chadwick, *The Popes and the European Revolution*, Oxford, 1981; J. Devlin, *The Superstitious Mind. French Peasants and the Supernatural in the Nineteenth Century*, New Haven, 1987; J. Sperber, *Popular Catholicism in Nineteenth-Century Germany*, Princeton, 1984 and W. Callahan, *Church, Politics and Society in Spain, 1750-1874*, Ithaca, 1984. Two excellent local studies of reaction in France are: B. Fitzpatrick, *Catholic Royalism in the Department of the Gard, 1815-1852*, Cambridge, 1983, and D. Higgs, *Ultraroyalism in Toulouse*, Baltimore, 1973. See also, R. Price, 'Legitimist opposition to the Revolution of 1830 in the French provinces', *Historical Journal*, 17, 1974, pp. 755-78. The author's own definition of reaction leads him to place several works on Germany titled 'conservative' in the category of reaction: Berdahl is essential, as are three contributions to L. E. Jones and J. N. Retallack, *Between Reform and Resistance: Studies in German Conservatism from 1789 to 1945*, Oxford, 1993: C. M. Clark, 'The politics of revival: pietists, aristocrats and the state Church in early nineteenth-century Prussia,' pp. 31-60. H. Beck, 'Conservatives and the Social Question in Nineteenth Century Prussia,' pp. 61-94; W. Schwentker, 'Victor Aimé Huber and the Emergence of Social Conservatism', pp. 123-56. There is very little on reaction, specifically, for the Italian states, despite its central importance to the period. A superb example of what can be done is A. J. Reinermann, 'The failure of popular counter-revolution in Risorgimento Italy: the case of the Centurions, 1831-1847', *Historical Journal*, 34, 1991, pp. 21-41. See also his *Metternich and the Papacy*. There is no comprehensive study of Carlism in English, although J. F. Coverdale, *The Basque Phase of Spain's First Carlist War*, Princeton, 1984, is good within its chosen limits and on local background. G. Brenan, *The Spanish Labyrinth*, Cambridge, 1991 edn is remarkable, if general. Those with French but not Spanish can learn much from F. Lafage, *L'Espagne de la Contre-Révolution*, Paris, 1993, while Spain has produced two massive - and opposing - studies in A. Bullón de Mendoza, *La Primera Guerra Carlista*, Madrid, 1992; and J.-C. Clemente, *Historia General del Carlismo*, Madrid, 1992. The best, recent study of the leading theorists of reaction is G. Gengembre, *La Contre-Révolution, ou l'historie désespérante*, Paris, 1989, although it tends to focus more on the Revolution.

By contrast, radicalism has a vast, impressive literature.

A good introduction remains A. Spitzer, *Old Hatreds and Young Hopes: the French Carbonari against the Bourbon Restoration*, Cambridge, Mass., 1971. A classic regional study, now in English, is M. Agulhon, *The Republic in the Village*, Cambridge, Eng. trans., 1982. On Italy, C. M. Lovett, *The Democratic Movement in Italy, 1830-1845*, Cambridge, Mass., 1982. On Germany, the relevant sections of J. L. Snell, *The Democratic Movement in Germany, 1789-1914*, Princeton, 1976. K. H. Wergel, 'Restoration radicals and "organic liberalism": Einheit-Freiehit reconsidered,' *Canadian Journal of History*, 12, 1978, pp. 299-323. E. Christiansen, *The Origins of Military Power in Spain, 1800-1854*, Oxford, 1967, is the best study in English of the Spanish radicals, and broader than its title suggests. On Britain, see J. Hamburger, *Intellectuals in Politics: J.S. Mill and the Philosophic Radicals*, London, 1965, and the collected writings of J. Dinwiddy, *English Radicalism*, Oxford, 1993. E. R. Royle, *Radical Politics, 1790-1900: Religion and Unbelief*, London, 1971, and with J. Walvin, *English Radicals and Reformers 1760-1848*, Brighton, 1982, are thoughtful introductions. Many studies of the 1848 revolutions focus on radicalism and set these events in the wider context of the Restoration period. J. Sperber, *Rhineland Radicals*, Princeton, 1991. P. H. Noyes, *Organisation and Revolution. Working-Class Association in the German Revolutions of 1848-1849*, Princeton, 1966. L. O'Boyle, 'The Democratic Left in Germany, 1848,' *Journal of Modern History*, 33, 1961, pp. 374-83. P. Ginsborg, *Daniel Manin and the Venetian Revolution of 1848-49*, Cambridge, 1979. J. Rath, *The Viennese Revolution of 1848*, Austin, 1957. J. V. Polišensk , *Aristocrats and the Crowd in the Revolutionary Year 1848*, Albany, Eng. trans., 1980. I. Deak, *The Lawful Revolution: Louis Kossuth and the Hungarians, 1848-1849*, New York, 1979.

There is also a large body of work on socialism, in all its forms. The best general guide is still G. Litcheim, *The Origins of Socialism*, New York, 1969. Also see K. Taylor, *Henri de St. Simon*, New York, 1975; F. Manuel, *The Prophets of Paris*, Cambridge, Mass., 1962; C. G. Moses, 'St Simonian men - St Simonian women: the transformation of feminist thought in 1830s France,' *Journal of Modern History*, 54, 1982, pp. 240-67. E. Berenson, *Populist Religion and Left-Wing*

Politics in France, 1830-1852, Princeton, 1984. P. N. Stearns, *Priest and Revolutionary: Lammenais,* New York, 1967. C. H. Johnson, *Utopian Communism in France: Cabet and the Icarians, 1839-1851,* Ithaca, 1974. A. Spitzer, *The Revolutionary Theories of Louis Auguste Blanqui,* New York, 1957. On the artisans see: W. H. Sewell, *Work and Revolution in France,* Cambridge, 1980; R. J. Bezucha, *The Lyon Uprising of 1834,* Cambridge, 1974; M. L. S. McDougall, *The Artisan Republic: Revolution, Reaction and Resistance in Lyon, 1848-1851,* Montreal, 1984. J. Rancière, *The Nights of Labour: the Workers' Dream in Nineteenth-Century France,* Philadelphia, Eng. trans., 1989. P. Amman, *Revolution and Mass Democracy: the Paris Club Movement of 1848,* Princeton, 1975, is valuable on the split between radicals and socialists. For a local study across the whole period, J. Merriman, *Red City: Limoges and the French Nineteenth Century,* Oxford, 1985. O. J. Hammen, *The Red '48ers: Karl Marx and Fredrich Engels,* New York, 1969, sets the Marxist leaders in a wider political context; its critique was ahead of its time.

Nationalism is a vast topic and many of the works cited already deal with aspects of it. The newest life of Mazzini, by D. Mack-Smith, New Haven, 1994 prefers to see his subject as a radical or liberal, and is very admiring. The classic work in Italian remains F. Della Peruta, *Mazzini e i rivoluzionari italiani: il 'partito d'azione' 1830-1845,* Milan, 1974. On Germany see, R. H. Thomas, *Liberalism, Nationalism and the German Intellectuals 1822-1847,* Cambridge, 1951. H. Schulze, *The Course of German Nationalism: from Frederick the Great to Bismarck 1763-1867,* Cambridge, Eng. trans., 1991, is a major study. W. J. Brazill, *The Young Hegelians,* New Haven, 1970. On Russia, N. Riasinovsky, *Nicholas I and Official Nationality in Russia, 1825-1855,* Berkeley, 1959. idem, *A parting of the Ways. Government and the Educated Public in Russia, 1801-1855,* Oxford, 1976. M. B. Petrovich, *The Emergence of Russian Panslavism,* New York, 1956. On the Habsburg Monarchy see: J. Zacek, *Palacký: the Historian as Scholar and Nationalist,* New York, 1970; K. Hitchens, *The Rumanian National Movement in Transylvania, 1780-1849,* Oxford, 1969; S. Pech, *The Czech Revolution of 1848,* Chapel Hill, 1969. On Poland see: A. Walicki, *Philosophy and Romantic Nationalism. The case of Poland,* Oxford, 1982. On Ireland, D. Gwynn, *Young Ireland and 1848,* Cork, 1949. T. Garvin, *Politics and Nationalism in Ireland,* London, 1981. D. Boyce, *Nationalism in Ireland,* London, 1980.

There is no general study of the revolutions of 1821, although the struggle for Greek independence has produced some fine studies: D. Dakin, *The Greek Struggle for Independence, 1821-1833*, London, 1973. R. Clegg, ed., *The Struggle for Greek Independence*, London, 1973. The only general work on 1830 is C. H. Church, *Europe in 1830*, London, 1983, which is a valuable source for Belgium, above all. On France, D. Pinkney, *The French Revolution of 1830*, Princeton, 1972 and J. Merriman, ed., *1830 in France*, New York, 1976, are indispensable. See also P. Pilbeam, 'The "three glorious days": the Revolution of 1830 in provincial France', *Historical Journal*, 26, 1983, pp. 831-44. In the huge literature on 1848, J. Sperber, *The European Revolutions of 1848-1851*, Cambridge, 1994, is by far the best general account, although P. Robertson, *Revolutions of 1848: a social history*, Princeton, 1952, and P. N. Stearns, *1848: the Revolutionary Tide in Europe*, New York, 1974, are also useful. F. Fejtö, ed., *Opening of an Era, 1848*, New York, 1949, is a stimulating collection of essays, and L. Namier, *1848: the Revolution of the Intellectuals*, London, 1971 edn is still thought-provoking.

Important national studies not mentioned elsewhere are: M. Agulhon, *The Republican Experiment, 1848-1852*, Cambridge, Eng. trans., 1983, R. Price, *The Second French Republic. A Social History*, London, 1972; J. Merriman, *The Agony of the Republic: the Repression of the Left in Revolutionary France, 1848-1851*, New Haven, 1978; all on France. R. Price, *1848 in France*, London, 1975, is a good collection of documents. For Germany, F. Eyck, *The Frankfurt Parliament 1848-1849*, London, 1968. D. Mattheisen, 'Liberal constitutionalism in the Frankfurt Parliament of 1848: an inquiry based on Roll-Call analysis', *Central European History*, 12, 1979, pp. 124-42. In German, the excellent W. Siemann, *Die deutsche Revolution von 1848/49*, Frankfurt, 1985, fills a gap at least as well as Agulhon for France. There is no recent, single monograph on the Italian revolutions of 1848-49, in Italian or English.

Index

absolutism 22–7, 54–5
adelfia 41
Agulhon, Maurice 73, 85–6
Alexander I, Tsar of Russia 39, 40, 41, 102
Amicizia Cattolica 60
Anderson, Benedict 91
artisans 82–3
Austria 13, 14, 16
conservatism 23
and Germany 11–12
nationalism 92
Tyrol revolt 54
Azeglio, Cesare, Marchese d' 60–1, 64

Baden 12, 13, 27–8, 31, 32
Balbo, Prospero 27
Balkan States 102, 109
Barcelona 83–4
Bavaria 12, 13, 22, 27–8, 32
Belgium 27, 45–6, 72, 102, 117
Bentham, Jeremy 127
Bernetti, Cardinal 62–3
Berry, Charles, Duc de 111
Besson, Hyacinthe 73
Bismarck, Prince Otto von 82, 89
Blanc, Louis 88–9, 97
Blanqui, Auguste 76–7
Boeckh, August 100

Bologna 42, 68
Bonald, Louis 57, 58–9
Breuilly, John 92, 101
Brinton, Crane 115–16
Britain
Catholic Emancipation 25, 44, 94, 102, 112
conservatism 24–5
First Reform Act 43, 44, 94, 112, 113
liberalism 35, 43, 46
nationalism 91, 93–5
parliamentarianism 17–18, 47–8, 93–4
radicalism 72, 75, 77
and Spain 108, 109
suffrage 71–2
Tories 24–5
Brougham, Henry Peter, 1st Baron 71, 75
Buonarotti, Filippo 41, 113
bureaucracy 23
Napoleonic 9, 14
Prussia 21–2, 23–4
Burke, Edmund 57
Byron, George Gordon, 6th Baron 102–3

Cabet, Étienne 81, 84, 85–6
Calderari 21, 62

141